CW00543999

SEVERN VALLEY RAILWAY

A VIEW FROM THE PAST

MICHAEL A. VANNS

Contents

First published 1998

ISBN 0 7110 2599 1

Published by Ian Allan Publishing

an imprint of Ian Allan Publishing Ltd, Terminal House, Station Approach, Shepperton, Surrey TW17 8AS.
Printed by Ian Allan Printing Ltd, Riverdene Business Park, Molesey Road, Hersham, Surrey KT12 4RG.

Code: 9809/B

Previous page:
A beautifully maintained Arley station on 24 September 1955, with ex-GWR 2-6-2T No 8105 arriving with a southbound train.
F. W. Shuttleworth (AO97)

Above:
Coalport station was typical of all the village stations on the Severn Valley line, the main buildings dating from 1861/2. At Coalport, the platform and loop on the right were added in 1895.
Ironbridge Gorge Museum Trust

Right:
The valley of the River Severn looking due west towards Shrewsbury in January 1967. In the foreground are the remains of Buildwas Abbey with the Severn Valley Railway branch running close by. Buildwas Junction was beneath the aircraft.
Aerofilms (A159637)

Front cover:
Three Edwardian coloured postcards; top, a Shrewsbury-bound train at the foot of Benthall Edge, Ironbridge Gorge; bottom left, Bridgnorth station from Pan Pudding Hill; bottom right, Ironbridge & Broseley station. *Ironbridge Gorge Museum Trust*

Back cover, top:
Peckett, 0-4-0ST in the sidings of Ironbridge power stations on 13 October 1962. *Author's collection*

Back cover, bottom:
No 41240 approaching Bewdley from the north during 1963 with the line from Tenbury Wells alongside.
Michael Messing

Foreword

The stretch of the River Severn between Shrewsbury and Worcester is a beautiful unspoiled part of middle England. The Severn Valley Railway between Shrewsbury and Hartlebury was a beautiful stretch of line, and fortunately part of that route remains so today thanks to the efforts of railway enthusiasts. It is unusual to write about a Victorian single-track branch line and be able to say it is still alive. So although this story is about the Severn Valley line before preservation in the 1970s, it is heartening to know that almost half of that original line can still be visited and enjoyed 136 years after it opened.

Since the author came to Shropshire 20 years ago, the preserved Severn Valley Railway has been one of his most enjoyable retreats. The riverside walk between Highley and Arley remains a particular favourite, the keeper of many special memories. For 10 years in the 1980s he lived at Ironbridge within sight of the remains of the railway, and it was always satisfying to imagine the trains that had passed along that route over the years, although a little sad to think of the generations of men and women who had kept those trains running, a labour which leaves no tangible remains.

Although the author is a little further away from the Severn Valley line now, in Coalbrookdale, as he assembled the text of this book a poem kept coming to mind which seems to distil in a few concise words what branch lines used to mean to many people before motor transport took their place.

M. A. Vanns
Coalbrookdale, spring 1998

Alone, in silence, at a certain time of night,
Listening, and looking up from what I'm trying to write
I hear a local train along the Valley. And "There
Goes the one-fifty," think I to myself; aware
That somehow its habitual travelling comforts me,
Making my world seem safer, homelier, sure to be
The same tomorrow; and the same, one hopes, next year.
"There's peacetime in that train." One hears it disappear
With needless warning whistle and rail-resounding wheels.
"That train's quite like an old familiar friend," one feels

A Local Train of Thought, Siegfried Sassoon.

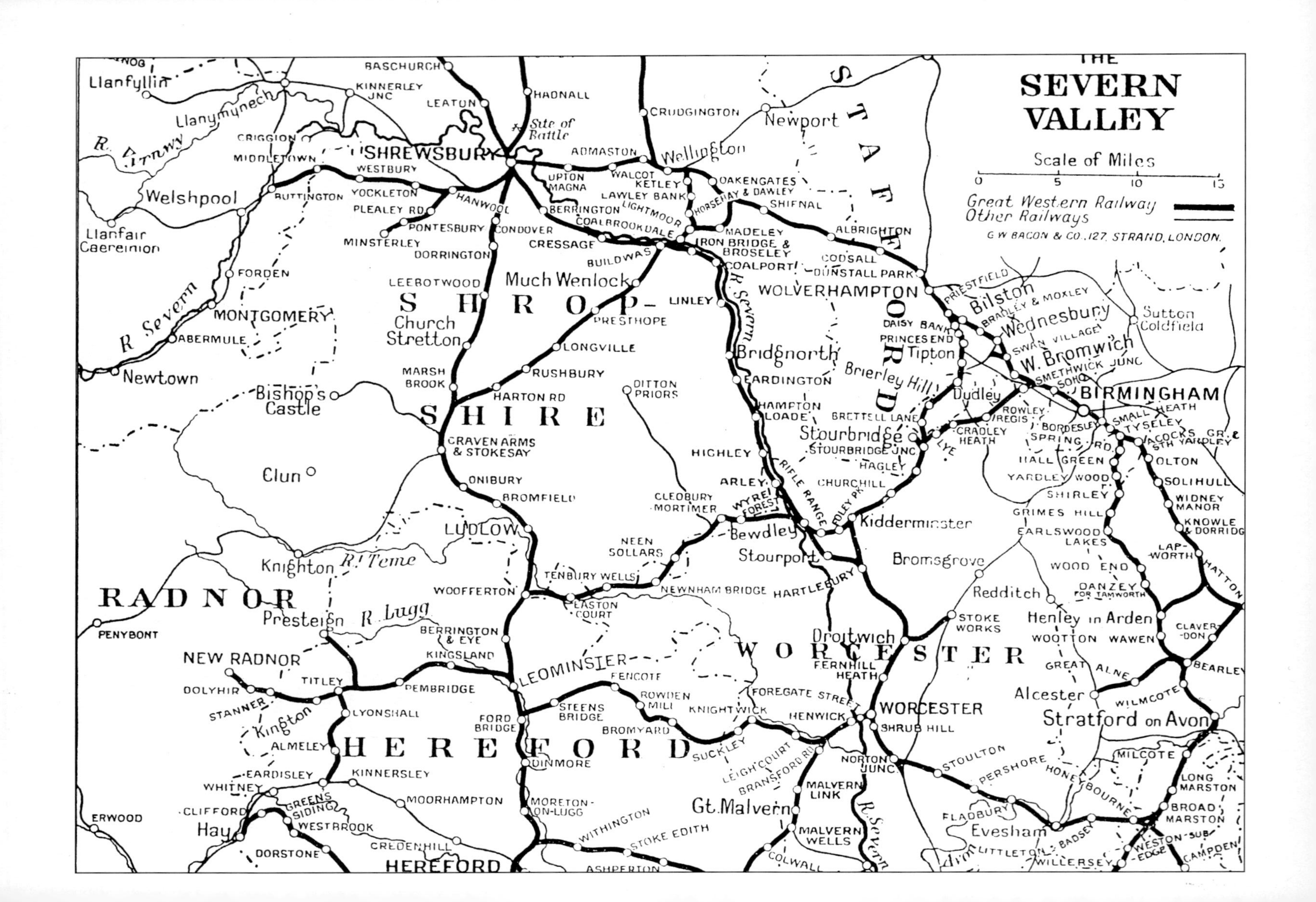
THE SEVERN VALLEY
Scale of Miles
0 5 10 15
Great Western Railway
Other Railways
G W BACON & CO. 127 STRAND, LONDON.
SHROPSHIRE
STAFFORD
WORCESTER
HEREFORD
RADNOR
SHREWSBURY
WOLVERHAMPTON
BIRMINGHAM
WORCESTER
HEREFORD
LEOMINSTER
LUDLOW
MONTGOMERY
Wellington
Newport
Bridgnorth
Kidderminster
Bewdley
Stourport
Stourbridge
Much Wenlock
Church Stretton
Bishop's Castle
Clun
Knighton
Presteign
Kington
Hay
Welshpool
Newtown
Llanfyllin
Llanymynech
Llanfair Caereinion
Droitwich
Bromsgrove
Redditch
Alcester
Stratford on Avon
Evesham
Gt. Malvern
Henley in Arden
Dudley
Tipton
Brierley Hill
Bilston
Wednesbury
W. Bromwich
Sutton Coldfield
R. Severn
R. Teme
R. Lugg
R. Vyrnwy
Avon
Site of Battle
NEW RADNOR
PENYBONT
BASCHURCH
KINNERLEY JNC
LEATON
HADNALL
CRUDGINGTON
ADMASTON
UPTON MAGNA
WALCOT
KETLEY
LAWLEY BANK
OAKENGATES
HORSEHAY & DAWLEY
SHIFNAL
ALBRIGHTON
CODSALL
DUNSTALL PARK
BERRINGTON
LIGHTMOOR
COALBROOKDALE
MADELEY
IRON BRIDGE & BROSELEY
COALPORT
CRESSAGE
BUILDWAS
CONDOVER
DORRINGTON
LEEBOTWOOD
HANWOOD
PONTESBURY
MINSTERLEY
PLEALEY RD
YOCKLETON
WESTBURY
BUTTINGTON
MIDDLETOWN
CRIGGION
FORDEN
ABERMULE
PRESTHOPE
LONGVILLE
RUSHBURY
HARTON RD
MARSH BROOK
CRAVEN ARMS & STOKESAY
ONIBURY
BROMFIELD
DITTON PRIORS
LINLEY
EARDINGTON
HAMPTON LOADE
HIGHLEY
ARLEY
WYRE FOREST
CLEOBURY MORTIMER
NEEN SOLLARS
TENBURY WELLS
EASTON COURT
NEWNHAM BRIDGE
WOOFFERTON
BERRINGTON & EYE
KINGSLAND
PEMBRIDGE
TITLEY
LYONSHALL
DOLYHIR
STANNER
ALMELEY
EARDISLEY
WHITNEY
CLIFFORD
GREENS SIDING
WESTBROOK
DORSTONE
ERWOOD
KINNERSLEY
MOORHAMPTON
CREDENHILL
FORD BRIDGE
DINMORE
MORETON-ON-LUGG
WITHINGTON
STOKE EDITH
ASHPERTON
STEENS BRIDGE
FENCOTE
ROWDEN MILL
BROMYARD
KNIGHTWICK
SUCKLEY
LEIGH COURT
BRANSFORD RD
FOREGATE STREET
HENWICK
SHRUB HILL
NORTON JUNC
MALVERN LINK
MALVERN WELLS
COLWALL
HARTLEBURY
FERNHILL HEATH
RIFLE RANGE
FOLEY PK
CHURCHILL
HAGLEY
STOURBRIDGE JUNC
BRETTELL LANE
LYE
CRADLEY HEATH
ROWLEY REGIS
DAISY BANK
PRINCES END
PRIESTFIELD
BRADLEY & MOXLEY
SWAN VILLAGE
SMETHWICK JUNC
SOHO
SMALL HEATH
TYSELEY
ACOCKS GR & STH YARDLEY
BORDESLEY
SPRING RD
HALL GREEN
YARDLEY WOOD
SHIRLEY
GRIMES HILL
EARLSWOOD LAKES
WOOD END
DANZEY FOR TAMWORTH
OLTON
SOLIHULL
WIDNEY MANOR
KNOWLE & DORRIDGE
LAPWORTH
HATTON
CLAVERDON
BEARLEY
WOOTTON WAWEN
GREAT ALNE
WILMCOTE
STOKE WORKS
STOULTON
PERSHORE
FLADBURY
HONEYBOURNE
MILCOTE
LONG MARSTON
BROAD MARSTON
LITTLETON BADSEY
WILLERSEY
WESTON-SUB-EDGE
CAMPDEN

The Severn Valley Railway
A View from the Past

Introduction

For almost exactly 101 years the Severn Valley branch of the Great Western Railway (GWR) provided a direct connection between Worcester and Shrewsbury, and from 1878 to 1963 it was also possible to run a train directly between the latter county town and Birmingham via Kidderminster. In reality the Severn Valley line was rarely used as a through route, and it is likely that few passengers travelled regularly from one end of the line to the other. Freight generated by the industries along the railway did flow out onto the wider national rail network, some of it to distant corners of the British Empire. But for most of its existence, the Severn Valley line was a picturesque, meandering, largely self-contained branch.

Three other GWR branch lines linked into it but none of these fed any significant quantity of traffic onto the Severn Valley branch and neither did it return any. There were the single-track lines from Madeley and Ketley Junctions both on the Birmingham-Wolverhampton-Shrewsbury main line combining at Lightmoor Junction to run into Buildwas Junction as a double line. There was the single-track branch from Marsh Farm Junction on the Shrewsbury-Hereford main line also running into Buildwas Junction. And lastly, from further south on the Shrewsbury-Hereford route there was the Woofferton Junction-Tenbury and Wyre Forest single branch line running into Bewdley. All these branches tended to direct traffic across the Severn Valley line, not on to it. At Buildwas Junction, for example, trains passed through between Wellington on the Birmingham-Wolverhampton-Shrewsbury main line and Craven Arms on the Shrewsbury-Hereford line, only straying onto the Severn Valley branch for the short distance necessary to cross from the north side of the junction at Buildwas to the south side. Likewise the flow of traffic on the Tenbury lines usually passed through Bewdley on its way between Stourbridge, Kidderminster, Woofferton and Hereford.

The Severn Valley line was at its most profitable in the 40 years between 1880 and 1920. In that period stations were lovingly maintained and well patronised, and private sidings were busy. The shops of the towns served by the railway were kept well stocked with mass-produced products from all over the country. Anything could be ordered and brought in by rail: fashionable shoes from Northamptonshire, fine net curtains from Nottinghamshire, or the best cutlery from Sheffield. Local ironmongers could be assured of a constant supply of all manner of items from screws and lamp glasses to varnish and paint from Birmingham and the Black Country. Grocers could rely on regular deliveries of fresh vegetables, fruit and flowers. And it was no longer necessary for publicans to brew their own beer, it could all be brought in by rail. The Severn Valley line also dealt with thousands of individual parcels coming into and going out of the area, and station yards and private sidings were just as busy dealing with the dispatch of locally manufactured products.

Of course, some stations and sidings were more remunerative than others and, looking at it dispassionately, the Severn Valley line was really only profitable in parts even in its late Victorian and Edwardian heyday. The 12½-mile stretch of line between Shrewsbury and Buildwas Junction contributed very little financially. In comparison, the 2½ miles between Buildwas and Coalport were very important for the company because of the industry on this section. The products of this area reached national and international markets and the railway was vital to their success. The 14 miles between Coalport and Highley were relatively barren ones except for the traffic you would expect to and from a town the size of Bridgnorth (5,865 people in 1891). By contrast, the three collieries immediately south of Highley (Highley, Kinlet and Billingsley) generated a very respectable volume of traffic. Two miles further south and Arley station was respectably quiet. Bewdley never generated the revenue that might have been expected from a junction station and at Stourport, 37½ miles from Shrewsbury, more traffic flowed eastwards away from the Severn Valley branch than onto it.

For a brief moment in the first decade of the 20th century, the Severn Valley line found itself at the forefront of GWR developments, with the inauguration of an omnibus service by road between Bridgnorth and Wolverhampton in 1904, and with the use of brand-new steam railcars on Bewdley-Kidderminster-Stourport services in 1905. But World War 1 changed everything, and by the late 1920s the line's best days were over as both passengers and the freight which had contributed to the prosperity of the line before the war began to desert the railway. It was not all decline. New industries did help counteract the losses: the West Midland Sugar Co's new factory at Kidderminster opened in 1925; the new electricity generating station at Buildwas Junction was brought on stream in 1932, Alveley Colliery feeding its output onto the railway in 1939, and the new connection to Stourport power station opened in 1940. All these helped to prolong the life of the branch after World War 2 but as passenger numbers collapsed and other traditional freight traffic was completely lost in the 1950s, closure was inevitable. Passenger trains stopped running between Shrewsbury and Bewdley in 1963 and barely seven years later British Rail withdrew passenger trains from the rest of the route.

Fortunately, today it is still possible to enjoy a journey along almost half the original length of the Severn Valley branch, and for those who wish to know a little more about the history of what remains and how the whole line appeared before preservation, the following should make an interesting journey.

Left:
On the afternoon of 22 August 1963, only 18 days before the passenger service was withdrawn between Shrewsbury and Bewdley, No W55018 stops at Jackfield Halt on its way to Shrewsbury.
F. W. Shuttleworth

The Severn Valley Railway
A View from the Past

1. Promotion and Construction

The Severn Valley Railway started life in the 'Railway Mania' years of the middle 1840s, a time when railway surveyors were trekking over every part of the country seeking out the best routes for main lines. The valley of the River Severn through Worcestershire and Shropshire was an obvious natural corridor along which a railway could be built. All that was needed was a reason for building such a line, and in the end two companies deposited plans supported by what they believed were good reasons for pushing a railway up the valley.

One of these companies was the Oxford & Worcester Extension & Chester Junction Railway. Planned in 1845 as a broad gauge extension of the proposed Oxford, Worcester & Wolverhampton Railway, it confidently declared that its line would be a vital link '...in the chain that will connect Liverpool with Bristol, the grand trunk of the west of England...'. As to the benefits of local traffic, it singled out '...the iron, coal, and earthenware works at Broseley and other places; the agricultural produce brought to Stourport market; [and] the inexhaustible fields of coal and mines of iron ore in the vicinity of Colebrook Dale [sic], Ironbridge, and the districts to the east of Shrewsbury generally'.

At first the proposed line was to run up the Severn Valley from Worcester through Bewdley and Bridgnorth to what was later called the Ironbridge Gorge. There the main line was to continue northwards up the Coalbrookdale valley to Wellington and on to Chester, whilst a branch was to continue eastwards to Shrewsbury. By the time the final plans were submitted to Parliament the branch between Ironbridge and Shrewsbury had been dropped and the main line route modified to run not through Coalbrookdale, but two miles further east through Stirchley to Wellington and Chester.

This change of plan was typical of the manoeuvring of companies during the Railway Mania, and in this case it was probably due to another concern — the Shropshire Union Railway & Canal Co — having designs on the same area. Amongst its list of 70 provisional directors were Richard Darby and Barnard Dickenson of the famous Coalbrookdale Works. The engineers of the railway were William Cubitt, Robert Stephenson and William Alexander Provis. Initially it was planned to build a line parallel with the River Severn only from Worcester through Bewdley and Bridgnorth to Coalport where it would turn northwards to Wellington to join the company's proposed Shrewsbury, Wellington and Stafford line. However, the final route surveyed in 1846 by Robert Stephenson and Frederick Swanwick (who were involved with many Midlands railway projects), included an extension from Coalport to Shrewsbury as well as a branch through Coalbrookdale. The plans and sections of this railway were presented from north to south. Consequently, the main line was to leave the planned Shrewsbury &

Severn Valley
RAILWAY.

NOTICE IS HEREBY GIVEN,
THAT A
PUBLIC
MEETING
of the Inhabitants of Bewdley, Stourport, and Neighbourhood,
is appointed to be held at the
TOWN HALL,
BEWDLEY,
On TUESDAY, APRIL 15th, 1856,
at 12 o'clock at noon, at which SIR SAMUEL MORTON PETO, Baronet, (the Chairman of the Severn Valley Railway Company,) will be present to explain the present position of the undertaking, when all persons interested in the same are requested to attend.

JAMES COLE,
Mayor of Bewdley.

Bewdley, 5th April, 1856.

T. E. DALLEY, PRINTER, BEWDLEY.

BRIDGNORTH.
SEVERN VALLEY
RAILWAY.

Notice is hereby given,
THAT A
PUBLIC MEETING
of the Inhabitants of this Town and Neighbourhood is appointed to be held at the
TOWN HALL,
BRIDGNORTH.
On Thursday, March 27th, 1856
at 12 o'clock at noon, at which SIR SAMUEL MORTON PETO, Baronet, (the chairman of the Directors of the said proposed Railway,) the Borough Members, and others, will attend to explain the present position of the undertaking.

JAMES B. GRIERSON,
MAYOR.

Bridgnorth, March 20th, 1856.

Above and above right:
Nearly three years after obtaining its original Act of Parliament, and with no immediate prospect of construction work starting, the Severn Valley Railway Co tried to rally support at public meetings in Bridgnorth and Bewdley.
Shropshire Records & Research (4001/Misc/4)

Birmingham Railway just north of the Abbey Church in Shrewsbury and run a little over 40 miles southwards along the Severn Valley to Stourport, where a branch was projected to Kidderminster, the main line continuing past Hartlebury to parallel the river again all the way to Worcester where it was to join the planned Oxford, Worcester & Wolverhampton Railway. The first branch in the Ironbridge Gorge was planned to cross the river half a mile west of the Iron Bridge running up the Coalbrookdale valley, past the ironworks there, to join the proposed Shrewsbury & Birmingham Railway branch. The second branch was also planned to cross the river from the south to the north bank but this time a mile and a half east of the Iron Bridge. The line was to run northwards past the blast furnaces of the Madeley Wood Co at Blists Hill just north of Coalport to Madeley, where it was expected to join the same Shrewsbury & Birmingham Railway branch line. Apart from these branches, the first few miles out of Shrewsbury and the last few miles south of Hartlebury, the route was the same as that later occupied by the Severn Valley branch of the West Midlands Railway (later to become part of the Great Western Railway) — the subject of this book.

Of the Shropshire Union Railway & Canal Co's many plans, only its Shrewsbury-Wellington-Stafford section of railway passed successfully through the Parliamentary committee stages in the Commons and the

modification before Col Yolland of the Railway Inspectorate of the Board of Trade would allow the branch to be opened to the public. After his first inspection in December 1861 he returned on 15 January the following year and reported that he was satisfied with the changes and would sanction the line's opening.

At 11.30am on Friday 31 January 1862 a train of 22 carriages departed from Worcester (Shrub Hill) station carrying Lord Shelbourne, Chairman of the GWR; Col George Cecil Weld Forester, MP for Wenlock and Chairman of the Severn Valley Railway; A. C. Sherriff, General Manager of the West Midlands Railway; John Fowler and his assistant H. O. Bridgeman; the contractors Brassey and Field, and various other dignitaries. Stopping at every station to be greeted by cheering crowds the train finally reached Shrewsbury at 2pm. Twenty minutes later with three more carriages and an extra engine it made its way back to Bridgnorth where a public dinner was laid on at the Assembly Room.

The following day regular passenger trains started to run — just three return trips over the whole line with an extra 9am Bridgnorth-Shrewsbury train and a return working leaving the county town at 5.45pm and arriving at Bridgnorth at 6.55pm. (For the first few months there was no Sunday service.) A journey stopping at all stations between Shrewsbury and Hartlebury took 5-10min over 2hr at a creditable average of 20mph for a railway still being 'run-in'. A week later on Tuesday 11 February another celebratory dinner was held in the George Hotel, Bewdley, attended by most of the party who had travelled on the inaugural train on the last day of January, and with toasts and much verbosity the Severn Valley branch of the West Midlands Railway was officially launched.

No sooner were the first trains making their leisurely way along the valley, than the Board of the Severn Valley Railway was busily drafting the terms of another agreement with the West Midlands Railway which was ratified by Parliament in July 1862. One of the clauses stated that the GWR was given the option to buy the Severn Valley Railway Co before the end of 1871, but before this happened the West Midlands Railway itself was taken over by the GWR in August 1863. Full amalgamation of the Severn Valley Railway Co with the GWR (whereby the preference shares in the former were exchanged for consolidated preference stock in the GWR) finally came on 1 July 1872 and from then on the branch became firmly part of God's Wonderful Railway.

Right:
Although this photograph probably dates from the 1870s, it shows Bridgnorth station as it looked when the line opened. The only obvious change since then was the replacement of the double-arm semaphore with separate home and starting signals (two of which are just visible in the background). The goods yard is crowded with wagons, which must have made shunting and marshalling very difficult. Notice also the large amount of timber opposite the goods shed. *Mrs M. Rutter*

The Severn Valley Railway

A View from the Past

2. Locomotives

When the West Midlands Railway was formed in 1860, it inherited a number of steam locomotives from its constituent companies. The new organisation had taken delivery of only a few of its own engines when the Severn Valley line opened at the beginning of 1862 and, consequently, as these new machines were undoubtedly allocated to main line duties, the branch was operated with a variety of locomotives from the Oxford, Worcester & Wolverhampton, the Newport, Abergavenny & Hereford, and the Worcester & Hereford railways. Amazingly, of these engines that are known to have worked over the Severn Valley line, photographs of a number of them have survived and they are reproduced in this chapter. Many of these locomotives finished their working lives on the line reboilered and often heavily rebuilt, by which time, although they remained handsome machines and were spotlessly turned out, they must have looked old-fashioned compared to the main line express locomotives they encountered at their home sheds of Shrewsbury or Worcester.

For passenger duties, engines of the 2-4-0 wheel arrangement remained the stable motive power until World War 1, supplemented occasionally by 0-4-2s and 0-6-0s, the latter used mostly on goods trains. In the decade

Below:
GWR 2-4-0 No 151 was a familiar sight on the line until 1920. *Locomotive Publishing Co/Ian Allan*

Above:
GWR 2-4-0 No 189 was built by E. B. Wilson & Co of Leeds in 1855 for the Oxford, Worcester & Wolverhampton Railway and rebuilt at Hereford in July 1864. It was this engine which left the rails on 20 June 1867 when departing from Bridgnorth station with the 10.55am Shrewsbury-Hartlebury passenger train. The cause of the accident was attributed to the locomotive not having been properly balanced on leaving Worcester works. No one was hurt and the locomotive survived to be rebuilt again in July 1882 before withdrawal in March 1886. *Locomotive Publishing Co/Ian Allan*

Below:
GWR 2-4-0 No 192 was also built by Wilson & Co in 1855 but for the Newport, Abergavenny & Hereford Railway. The locomotive was rebuilt in 1874 and again in 1890 into the form shown in this photograph. Shedded at Worcester, No 192 worked regularly on the Severn Valley line until she was withdrawn in 1903. *Locomotive Publishing Co/Ian Allan*

immediately before war broke out, a number of services at the southern end of the Severn Valley line were worked by steam railcars and then at the beginning of the 1920s, 'auto cars' took over these duties some working as far as Bridgnorth as the following extract from the October 1922 GWR Working Timetable shows:

Right:
GWR 0-4-2T No 1440 and auto-trailer at Arley station on 7 September 1932. *Selwyn Pearce Higgins Collection (Q21), National Railway Museum*

Below right:
GWR 4-4-0 No 3454 *Skylark* was one of a few 'Bulldog' class locomotives that appeared on Severn Valley branch passenger trains in World War 2. *Locomotive Publishing Co/Ian Allan*

Down Trains									
Kidderminster	5.30am								
Hartlebury	-			8.20	10.05	2.45	3.53		7.45
Stourport	-	7.19	8.26	8.27	10.12	2.53	4.00	6.5	7.52
Bewdley (a)	5.38	7.25	8.33	8.35	10.18	3.00	4.05	6.11	7.58
(d)	5.41								8.18
Arley (a)	5.47								8.25
(d)	5.50								
Highley	5.56								8.32
Hampton Loade									8.39/40
Bridgnorth									8.48
Up Trains									
Highley		6.05am							
Arley		6.15							
Bewdley (a)	6.22			9.14*		11.48*	1.42*		
(d)	6.35	7.06	7.55	9.17	11.00	11.51	2.10	3.22	5.56
Stourport		7.13	8.02	9.24	11.08	11.58	2.17	3.30	6.02
Hartlebury			8.08	9.31	11.15	12.04	2.24	3.37	
Kidderminster	?								
Worcester						12.15			
Bridgnorth		8.55pm							
Hampton Loade		9.05							
Highley			9.11						
Arley			9.17						
Bewdley (a)		9.24							
(d)	7.13pm*	9.38							
Stourport	7.19								
Hartlebury	7.26								
Kidderminster		?							

**From Kidderminster*

At the very end of the 1920s, brand new 2-6-2 tanks of the '45xx' class were drafted in to work the remaining passenger trains and proved popular engines on these turns. In October 1927 Nos 5505/6/7 were allocated to Kidderminster shed, joined in the following month by No 5508. It was No 5508 which came to grief with its train just north of Bridgnorth tunnel on 13 January 1928. At 8.31pm whilst travelling at 45-50mph, rotten sleepers gave

BOOKING OFFICE

way under the rocking locomotive which then tore up a long section of track, derailing itself and the three bogie carriages in tow.

Fortunately, the train remained upright and no one was injured. The accident did not stop the use of 2-6-2 tanks on the line, and they soon became the usual motive power for both passenger and freight work until the late 1950s. During World War 2 when the line was used as a diversionary route, larger 2-6-2 tanks of the '51xx' class appeared along with ex-Cambrian Railways 0-6-0s and even 'J25' 0-6-0s on loan from the London & North Eastern Railway. On passenger trains, a number of William Dean's beautifully proportioned 'Duke' class 4-4-0s were to be seen, a generation removed from their glory days at the turn of the century on the main line out of Paddington. Alongside these engines, a number of ageing 'Bulldog' 4-4-0s also finished their days on the Severn Valley line. No 3353 *Pershore Plum*, No 3453 *Seagull*, and No 3454 *Skylark* were familiar wartime visitors.

In 1936 the GWR's new stylish diesel railcars began to work some of the services between

Above:
GWR 4-4-0 No 3254 *Cornubia* of the 'Duke' class was also a regular on wartime passenger trains between Shrewsbury and Hartlebury.
Locomotive Publishing Co/Ian Allan

Above right:
Typical of the motive power for passenger trains on the Severn Valley line for many years, ex-GWR 2-6-2T No 4129 leaving Arley station on 24 March 1962 with the 12.10pm Bridgnorth-Hartlebury (SO) train.
B. S. Moone

Right:
Ex-GWR diesel railcar No 7 was built in 1935 and could accommodate 70 seated passengers. It is seen here at Arley on 24 September 1955 forming the 1pm from Bewdley to Shrewsbury. *F. W. Shuttleworth*

Kidderminster, Hartlebury and Stourport, and after the war they started to travel the full length of the line. Those passenger turns which remained steam-hauled as well as all the goods trains were in the hands of locomotives from both Shrewsbury (Coleham) (84G) and Kidderminster (85D) sheds, the latter

4129

providing most of the motive power by the 1950s. 2-6-2 tanks remained the most common type, supplemented by a number of 0-6-0 pannier tanks and 2-6-0s on coal trains.

Because the Severn Valley line had been part of the Great Western Railway since 1872 and that company had survived the Grouping of the railways in 1923, and furthermore because its traditions had also passed intact into the Western Region of British Railways in 1948, there was a very strong continuity about the operation of the branch, and the engines and rolling stock employed. It was only when steam locomotives were being phased out that the character of the line changed noticeably. By the 1960s the ex-GWR locomotives had been largely displaced by ex-LMS and BR standard types and the ex-GWR railcars replaced by British Railways' less glamorous equivalents. It was these machines that maintained the service until the line closed as a through route in September 1963 with one notable and appropriate exception. The very last British Railways passenger train to run into Bridgnorth from the south on 8 September 1963 was hauled by two ex-GWR 0-6-0 pannier tanks — Nos 9624 and 4665. At the time it seemed a fitting conclusion to the line's history, but within only a few years Bridgnorth was to witness the arrival of a wonderful variety of main line steam locomotives from all the 'Big Four' (LMS, SR, LNER and GWR) railways, including the GWR's most powerful and impressive steam locomotive, a 'King' class 4-6-0.

Below:
Ex-GWR 0-6-0 pannier tank locomotives Nos 9624 and 4665 ready to depart southbound from Bridgnorth with the very last British Railways passenger train on a dull 8 September 1963. *Neil Clarke*

Right:
Ex-LMS 2-6-2T No 41207 represents the typical type of motive power used in the years immediately before British Railways stopped running passenger trains north of Bewdley. It is seen here on 22 August 1963 on a Kidderminster-bound passenger working at Bridgnorth. *F. W. Shuttleworth*

Below right:
Another regular in the closing years of the passenger service was BR railcar No W55018 photographed at Kidderminster station waiting to form an afternoon service to Shrewsbury on 22 August 1963.
F. W. Shuttleworth

41207

KNOWLE
W55018
2

3. The Route

Mileage along the Severn Valley branch was measured from Hartlebury (and these distances are noted below next to the relevant stations), but as the railway took its name from the River Severn which it followed for most of its course, often within a few hundred metres, it seems appropriate when describing the line to flow with the river generally from north to south.

Below:
The bay platform at the south end of Shrewsbury (General) station used by Severn Valley branch trains. Here, ex-LMS 2-6-2 No 41304 has just arrived with a train from Bridgnorth in August 1963.
Andrew Muckley

Shrewsbury (40½ miles)

Starting from Shrewsbury station, branch line trains used the Hereford line as far as Sutton Bridge Junction, where the Severn Valley line curved away to the southeast. Sutton Bridge Junction signalbox opened in 1913 to replace an earlier structure and is still in use at the time of writing (1998). The Severn Valley branch was double track for 18 chains (362m), the single line starting at Burnt Mill Junction signalbox brought into use at the beginning of 1894. This box was closed in February 1937 when the points there were motorised so they could be worked from Sutton Bridge Junction.

Above right:
The signalman at Sutton Bridge Junction on the Shrewsbury-Hereford main line hands the train (key) token to the fireman of ex-GWR 2-6-2T No 4114 as it heads down the Severn Valley line on 22 July 1963. *R. H. Robinson*

Right:
The fireman of an ex-GWR 0-6-0 pannier tank surrenders the token from Berrington to the signalman at Sutton Bridge Junction, Shrewsbury in 1953.
Russell Mulford

4114

SUTTON BRIDGE JUNCTION SIGNAL

Above:
Ex-GWR 2-6-0 No 7338 hauling an excursion train comes off the Severn Valley branch onto the Shrewsbury-Hereford line at Sutton Bridge Junction in the early 1950s. *Russell Mulford*

Below:
Three-quarters of a mile from Sutton Bridge Junction on the outskirts of Shrewsbury, ex-GWR 2-6-2T No 4178 is going well with the 1.45pm to Hartlebury on 24 September 1960. *Michael Mensing*

Berrington (36 miles)

Berrington was the first station out of Shrewsbury, four miles from the county town. When the line opened in 1862 the population of the village half a mile from the railway was just 772. This total included the staff and inmates of the Cross Houses Union Workhouse on the Shrewsbury-Much Wenlock turnpike only a few hundred metres from the station. The workhouse had been opened in 1834, and after enlargement in 1871 was capable of housing 550 'inmates'. By the end of the 19th century the number of potential railway customers from these two rural settlements had risen to 968, and in 1903 the resident stationmaster, Mr William Cleeton, issued just under 17,000 tickets.

Below:
The single-storey range at Berrington station was doubled in length in 1894 to incorporate a ladies' waiting room and WC shortly after the down loop and platform with shelter was opened. Ex-LMS 2-6-2T No 41209 waits with a down train bound for Shrewsbury on 24 August 1963. *Andrew Muckley*

Left:
Weighbridge buildings like this one at Berrington station were apparently provided at all Severn Valley line stations when the line opened in 1862.
Andrew Muckley

Below:
The young signalman at Berrington signalbox is still using his cloth in traditional GWR fashion just over two weeks before the last passenger trains were due to be withdrawn, and only four months before the box closed. *Andrew Muckley*

Right:
Cound Halt with ex-GWR 2-6-2T No 4147 approaching from the south in August 1963. The River Severn is behind the bushes on the left. *Andrew Muckley*

Cound Halt (33½ miles)

Two miles from Berrington the River Severn came within touching distance of the railway and here, sandwiched between it and the main road between Shrewsbury, Cressage and Much Wenlock, the GWR opened a single wooden platform on 4 August 1934, christening it Cound Halt. It was one of four similar halts opened along the Severn Valley line between the wars. They were meant to be the equivalent of bus stops and were part of a strategy to try and stem the haemorrhage of passengers away to road transport in this period. However, of all the halts, Cound must have been the most difficult to justify, because although it took its name from the nearest hamlet, it was of more use to fishermen than local residents who, by the time they had walked to the main road, were still a mile away from the new halt. We will never know just how many people used the platform, but it did remain open as a request stop until the line closed to passengers in September 1963.

Between Cound and Cressage the railway was almost straight and level over the widest part of the river's flood plain. To their left, passengers had a good view of Shropshire's isolated peak (407m above sea level) — The Wrekin — and in front of them the rising slopes of Wenlock Edge.

Cressage (32 miles)

Eight miles from Shrewsbury, Cressage was one of the original 1862 stations on the line, conveniently located immediately northwest of the village with a population of just 350. Strangely, as at Berrington (and a number of other Severn Valley line stations), the station buildings and sidings were on the eastern side of the railway furthest away from the village. This apparently illogical arrangement no doubt had something to do with the availability of land and perhaps the original double-track plans.

The line at Cressage was not doubled, however, until 1893/4 when a loop, signalbox and second platform were finally brought into use. The signalbox was built on the village side of the line and was equipped with a wheel to operate the four level crossing gates. Like the arrangement at Berrington which was authorised at the same time, a ground frame was provided to work the points at the end of the loop furthest from the signalbox; in the case of Berrington this was at the south end of the layout, whilst at Cressage the frame was located at the north end.

Between Cressage and the next station at Buildwas Junction, the railway kept to the edge of, and just above, the river's flood plain and like the Severn to the north, it gently meandered eastwards through unspoiled countryside. Half a mile before Buildwas Junction, the line passed only a few hundred metres to the south of the remains of Buildwas Abbey, built by the Cistercian Order in the second half of the 11th century. Development like this so close to an ancient monument would not be tolerated today. Architectural historian, Nikolaus Pevsner, drew attention to this particular example of cavalier Victorian construction in his first edition of *The Buildings of England: Shropshire* published in 1958, but rather undermined the validity of his comments by inaccurately accusing the railway of cutting off the abbey from the river, which it did not.

The setting of Buildwas Abbey was further compromised during World War 1 when a sand pit was opened directly opposite the ruin, and connected to the Severn Valley line by a short siding.

Below:
Cressage signalbox and level crossing photographed at the end of the 1950s. Opened in June 1894, the signalbox finally closed on 2 December 1963.
J. H. Moss

Above:
Cressage station looking towards Shrewsbury, a photograph taken in the first decade of the 20th century. *Ironbridge Gorge Museum Trust*

Below:
The same station almost 60 years later on 24 August 1963 with ex-LMS 2-6-2T No 41209 on a Shrewsbury-Bridgnorth train. *Andrew Muckley*

Buildwas Junction (28 miles)

Buildwas Junction was for the GWR what Trent Junction just south of Nottingham was for the MR — an interchange station in the middle of open countryside with no passenger access other than by train. Like Trent station opened in the same year as the Severn Valley line, Buildwas Junction station was simply a place where passengers could change trains. The station buildings were of the same design as those at Bewdley and Stourport, except that behind the structure at first-floor level was the single platform for trains to and from Much Wenlock. Trains serving this picturesque town started to run on the same day as the Severn Valley branch opened to passengers — 1 February 1862. The promotion of the Much Wenlock & Severn Junction Railway had been supported by the Severn Valley Railway Co in

Above right:
The Severn Valley line platforms at Buildwas Junction looking east in August 1963. Out of sight on the left is the single platform for Wellington and Much Wenlock trains. *Andrew Muckley*

Left:
Buildwas Junction, 1885. *Crown Copyright*

Right:
On the left-hand side of this photograph is the original crossing keeper's cottage on the Buildwas-Much Wenlock road with the recently opened (1906) bridge over the River Severn just visible in the background. The hut to the right is Buildwas Crossing Ground Frame. *Ironbridge Gorge Museum Trust*

Left:
The wooden sign with cast-iron letters on the up platform at Buildwas Junction. The words 'Craven Arms' used to occupy the space after 'Much Wenlock' but was removed when the passenger service beyond Much Wenlock was withdrawn on 31 December 1951. *Kidderminster Railway Museum*

1859, its support helping the former secure the Royal Assent on 21 July that year.

From 1 November 1864, trains also began to run into Buildwas from Coalbrookdale on the double tracks from Lightmoor Junction and the single lines from there to Madeley and Ketley junctions, both nearly five miles northeast of Buildwas (as the crow flies) on the main line between Birmingham, Wolverhampton and Shrewsbury.

The stretch of line between Buildwas and Lightmoor Junction had a complicated history. A single-track line from Madeley Junction to Lightmoor had been built by the Shrewsbury & Birmingham Railway and opened to goods traffic on 1 June 1854, two months before the railway became part of the GWR. Only a few miles to the west another single line was then constructed off the Shrewsbury & Birmingham line by the Wellington & Severn Junction

Left:
Buildwas Junction looking towards the Ironbridge Gorge from above the Wellington-Much Wenlock platform in 1932. Buildwas Junction signalbox can just be seen in the distance, having recently been extended to accommodate a larger lever frame. *Real Photographs (11750)*

Railway from Ketley Junction to the Horsehay ironworks. Opened to goods in May 1857, it was extended southwards the following year to join the Madeley Junction line at Lightmoor. The extensions into Coalbrookdale, southwest from Lightmoor and eastwards from Buildwas Junction, were built as two separate railways but opened on the same day — 1 November 1864 — as a double track through route. The construction of the section through the crowded industrial valley of Coalbrookdale was not easy and to take the line across the river to Buildwas Junction, John Fowler's bridge design used at Arley was used again. The substantial and impressive iron ribs, as for the Victoria Bridge at Arley, were cast at the nearby Dale works.

On 5 December 1864, only a month after the new Coalbrookdale line was carrying traffic, the Much Wenlock line was extended southwards along the foot of Wenlock Edge to limestone quarries at Presthope. Gradually this

Left:
Ex-GWR 2-6-2T No 4401 in the high-level platform at Buildwas Junction waiting with a train bound for Wellington whilst ex-GWR 2-6-2T No 4139 pauses with a train from Shrewsbury in the Severn Valley branch platform, August 1950.
Real Photographs (K947)/National Railway Museum

Above:
The wooden board on the Wellington-Much Wenlock platform at Buildwas Junction.
Kidderminster Railway Museum

Below:
The West Midlands Joint Electricity Authority's new power station under construction just north of Buildwas Junction in 1930.
Ironbridge Gorge Museum Trust

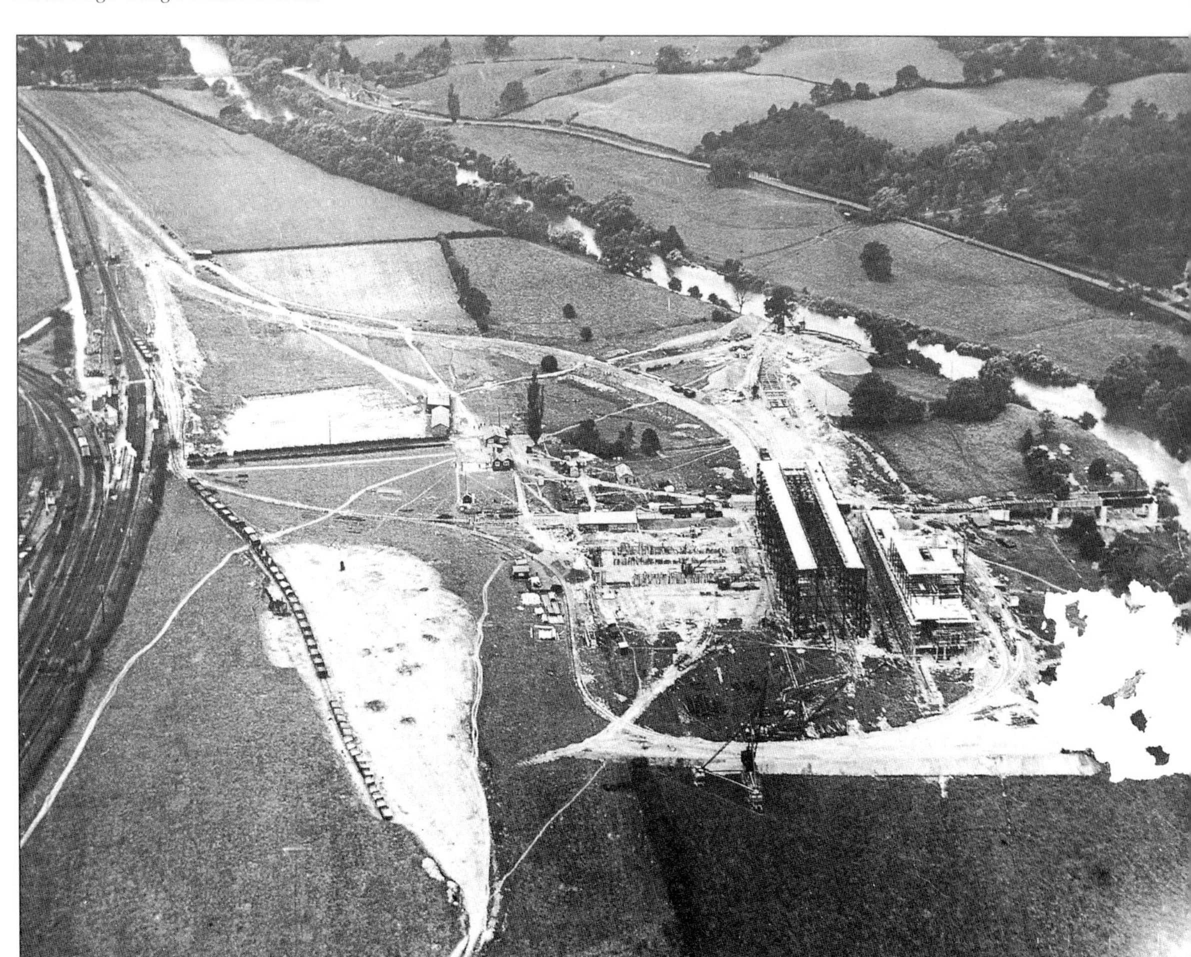

Above:
At the west end of the Wellington-Much Wenlock platform the fireman of ex-GWR 0-6-0 pannier tank No 9639 grapples with the water tower apparatus as the driver smiles for the camera on 21 July 1962. Ironbridge Power Station is in the background. *Leslie Sandler*

Above:
Ex-GWR 0-6-0 pannier tank No 8727 taking water at the end of the Severn Valley line up platform, Buildwas Junction on 6 September 1956 whilst working a southbound mixed goods train. *Neil Clarke*

brave single-track railway was pushed further to connect into other quarries, finally reaching a junction with the Shrewsbury-Hereford main line at Marsh Farm Junction which was brought into use on 16 December 1867.

Passenger traffic was always very light, but Buildwas Junction soon echoed to the sound of numerous limestone trains making their way northeastwards not only to the Coalbrookdale Co furnaces and to the Lilleshall iron and steel works four miles further north at Oakengates, but also to the numerous blast furnaces in South Staffordshire. The expanding Lilleshall Co ran its own limestone quarry near Presthope which extracted at its peak 1,000 tons of stone a week in 1900. Because of the

Right:
Retirement presentation at Buildwas Junction in 1958. The stationmaster Mr Toye (left) shakes hands with retiring yard foreman, Harry Davies (on the right). Between them in the centre of the photograph is Percy Griffiths, District Inspector.
Ironbridge Gorge Museum/Wellington Journal

amount of traffic passing through Buildwas Junction, the GWR had had to alter the original signalling there as early as 1873, erecting extra signals and working them from a fully interlocked lever frame. This arrangement lasted until 1888, when two new signalboxes were opened, one at the station and the other at the junction where the double-track Coalbrookdale line joined the single-track Severn Valley line.

It is unfortunate that there are apparently no photographs of limestone traffic passing through Buildwas Junction. This lack of interest contrasts markedly with the situation in the early 1930s, when hundreds of official photographs were taken during the building of the electricity generating station immediately to the north of Buildwas Junction station. Here in 1932, one of Britain's first 'super' electricity generating power stations started to supply electricity to the new National Grid. Plans for a power station dated back to 1924 when the Walsall Borough Council's Electricity Supply Department had inspected the site. These plans were adopted by the West Midlands Joint Electricity Authority in 1927 as part of an integrated regional and an embryonic national strategy initiated by the Government in the Electricity Supply Act of 1919 and reinforced when the Central Electricity Board was created by Act of Parliament in 1926. The site was chosen because of its railway connections and the close proximity of the river with more than adequate water for the cooling of the turbines. Building began in 1929 with most of the materials coming in by rail and on 13 October 1932 the official opening of the first part of the power station took place with dignitaries arriving on a special train from Paddington.

To control the modified layout and connections into the power station sidings a new 113-lever frame was installed in Buildwas signalbox and brought in to use on 9 December 1931. This signalbox was comparatively new, having replaced the two 1888 boxes in 1923. The power station was enlarged at the end of 1935 and again in the winter of 1938-9 when another boiler house with three distinctive steel chimneys was added to match the original building with its set of three. Initially between 500 and 600 tons of coal was brought in by rail every day, this rising gradually until 2,500 tons could be dealt with daily in the late 1950s. After World War 2 coal from Highley Colliery was supplemented by deliveries from Granville and Kemberton pits to the east of Oakengates. Coal also came from the Staffordshire coalfield, the trains marshalled at

Above:
A Wellington-bound diesel railcar at Buildwas Junction in 1961.
Russell Mulford

Right:
A view of the Albert Edward Bridge looking due west from Benthall Edge at the end of the 19th century. Far left in the background is Buildwas Junction.
Ironbridge Gorge Museum Trust

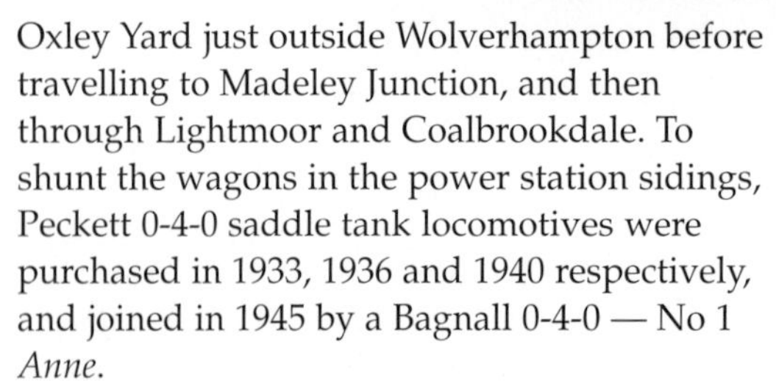

Oxley Yard just outside Wolverhampton before travelling to Madeley Junction, and then through Lightmoor and Coalbrookdale. To shunt the wagons in the power station sidings, Peckett 0-4-0 saddle tank locomotives were purchased in 1933, 1936 and 1940 respectively, and joined in 1945 by a Bagnall 0-4-0 — No 1 *Anne*.

By the beginning of the 1960s, plans were in hand for another state-of-the-art power station on the remaining land owned by the CEGB next to Buildwas Junction. Although the railway was a crucial consideration in the location of the new station, remaining the main artery for incoming coal and oil, the siting of Ironbridge 'B' actually hastened the end of the Severn Valley line as a through route between Shrewsbury, Kidderminster and Hartlebury. The new power station was constructed south of the railway and the easternmost one of four concrete cooling towers was built across the trackbed of the railway. Work began in the summer of 1963, the passenger service along the Severn Valley line ceased from 9 September 1963 and in May 1964 Buildwas Junction station was demolished to make way for the new coal-handling plant. To complete the power station story, the first electricity generated at Ironbridge 'B' to enter the National Grid did so on 11 June 1969, with the power station fully commissioned on 27 February 1970.

Moving on a mile from Buildwas Junction the Severn Valley line entered the neck of the Ironbridge Gorge running almost due west-east, its limestone cliffs rising steeply both sides of the river. For the next couple of miles, the railway clung tightly to the south side of the gorge with the river only a few hundred metres below. The landscape here was completely different to the rolling wide stretches of farmland which characterised the route between Shrewsbury and Buildwas. It was from here southwards that the Severn Valley line actually began to earn money.

By 1862, the fame of the Ironbridge and Coalbrookdale area (the valley and settlement just to the north of the river) was already an international one. The Coalbrookdale ironworks, controlled since 1708/9 by a dynasty of Quaker ironmasters named Darby, and John Wilkinson's works in nearby Broseley, had been in the forefront of technical developments for 100 years. Iron cylinders for Boulton & Watt's steam engines and cannon for the Napoleonic Wars were cast and bored in the local ironworks. Some of the first cast-iron rails to be used in this country, replacing wooden ones on the extensive network of local tram and railway lines, were laid in 1767, and in 1802 Richard Trevithick had turned to William Reynolds and the Coalbrookdale Co to fabricate his first railway (plateway) steam locomotive, two years before the more famous Penydarren locomotive ran.

Probably the most emotive symbol of the British Industrial Revolution was, and still remains, the Iron Bridge, cast by the Coalbrookdale Company and thrown over the river here between 1779 and 1781. However, when the Severn Valley Railway built its station within spitting distance of this famous bridge, the area was no longer in the vanguard of progress, and most of the 18th century's pioneering spirit had gone. The settlement which took its name from the Iron Bridge was transforming itself into a respectable Victorian town, the police station, for example, appearing in the same year as the railway. In Coalbrookdale the ironworks was turning to the production of decorative cast-iron garden furniture, civic fountains, etc, leaving the latest developments in steel fabrication to others.

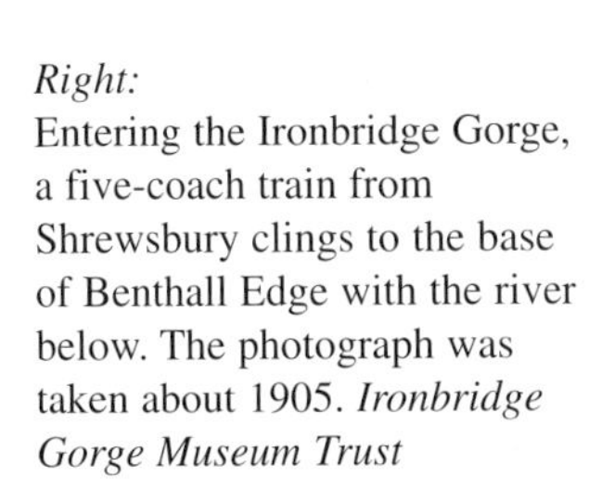

Right:
Entering the Ironbridge Gorge, a five-coach train from Shrewsbury clings to the base of Benthall Edge with the river below. The photograph was taken about 1905. *Ironbridge Gorge Museum Trust*

Ironbridge & Broseley (27miles)

At Ironbridge a considerable embankment and plateau with a massive retaining wall over 15m high had to be formed to accommodate the station site. Geography had dictated that the railway had to pass through the Ironbridge Gorge on the south side of the river and this meant that everyone in adjacent Ironbridge and Coalbrookdale was obliged to pay a toll for crossing the Iron Bridge each time they wanted to use the railway station. Consequently, although the population of Ironbridge (3,154) compared favourably with that of Bewdley (3,158) when the line opened, passengers and those traders using the goods facilities were in effect subject to additional charges every time they used the railway. The tolls on the Bridge were not removed until 1950. Coalbrookdale, of course, had its own station with full goods facilities on the Wellington-Much Wenlock line, and the Coalbrookdale Co had its own sidings off this branch.

Ironbridge station was perhaps of more use to those individuals and industries on the south side of the river. The town of Broseley just half a mile to the south of the station had a population of 4,724 in 1861 and although it was connected to the station by an extremely steep road — Bridge Bank — much traffic was generated. The encaustic and decorative tileworks established by Maw & Co in 1852 on Bridge Bank used the goods facilities extensively, a fact highlighted in October 1905 when the Board of Directors of the company agreed to give Mr Charles William Coldicott, the retiring stationmaster, a very generous £10 10s (£10.50) in consideration of '…his long connection with [the] Company, and his untiring courtesy…'. In Broseley itself, the long-established clay tobacco pipe manufacturing industry was given a new lease of life after the Severn Valley line opened because the GWR could not only bring in the best quality pipe clays from Devon and Cornwall faster and more cheaply than previously by river, but it could also transport the two most important firms' travellers the length and breadth of the country soliciting orders for pipes.

Below:
Ironbridge, 1902. *Crown Copyright*

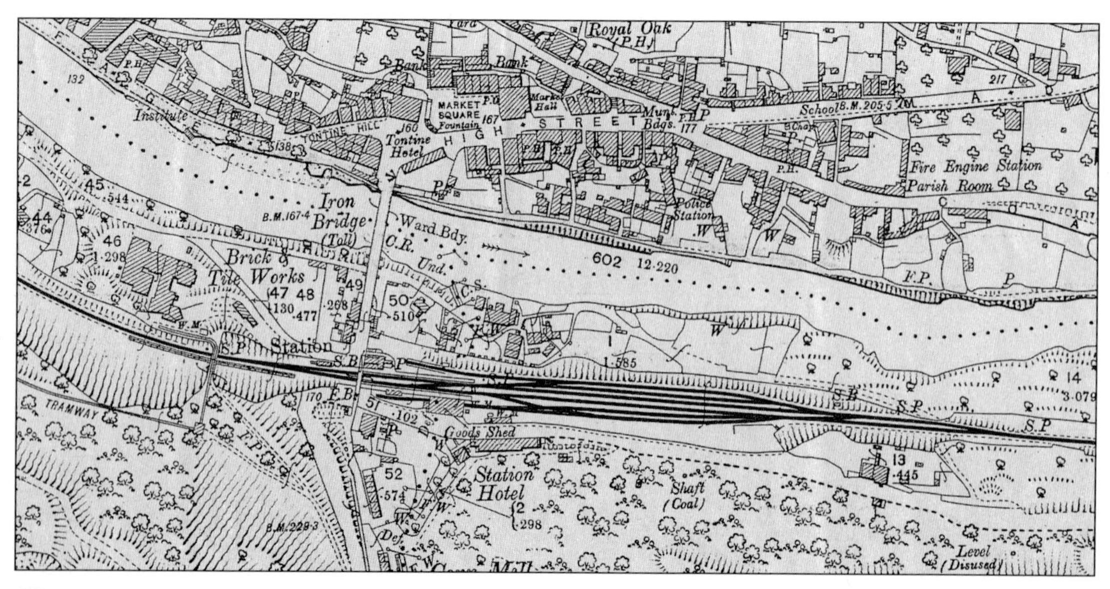

Above:
Ironbridge & Broseley station in the Edwardian period. The station building had no accommodation for a stationmaster and so was a modified version of the design used at Buildwas Junction, Bewdley and Stourport.
Shropshire Records & Research (B3939)

Right:
The signalbox at Ironbridge & Broseley was built in 1894 to the then standard GWR Type 5 design although it was slightly narrower than the signalboxes opened at Cressage and Berrington at the same time. *T. Blood Collection*

Further east along the railway in the less savoury district of Jackfield, the industries using locally dug clay also benefited from the arrival of the Severn Valley line. In the two miles between Ironbridge and Coalport stations, there were numerous brick and tile works. Jackfield Siding, which was provided for these firms, was three-quarters of a mile from Ironbridge station, and in one of the earliest surviving Working Timetables for the branch (1865) it is recorded that the 8.40am Shrewsbury goods, the 10.25am Dudley goods arriving at 2.25pm, and the 2.50pm from Hartlebury, due at 5.35pm, were all booked to stop for just 5min there. The sidings were progressively expanded so that by the end of

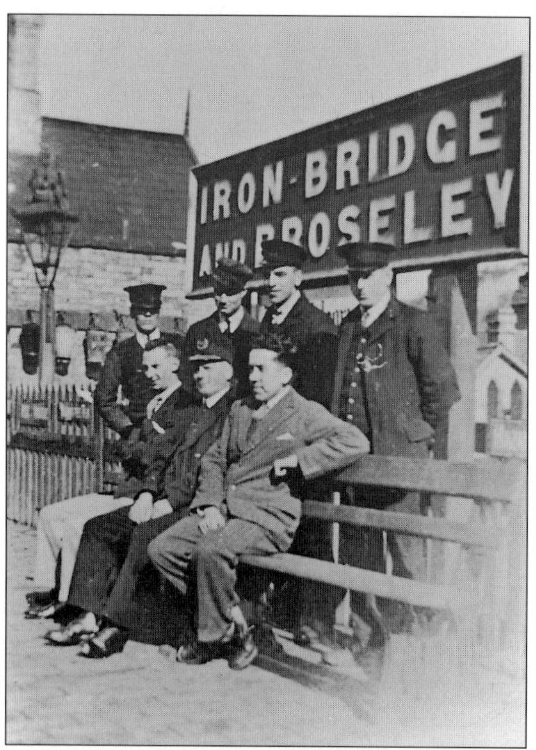

Above:
Ironbridge & Broseley station as it appeared in the first few years of the 20th century with a 2-4-0 engine waiting to leave with a Shrewsbury-bound train. The town of Ironbridge in the background was on the opposite side of the river to the station.
Ironbridge Gorge Museum Trust

Left:
The entire station staff photographed in 1933. Standing from left to right: Arthur Ansell, porter; Walter Dickens, lorry driver; Fred Jones, porter; and Bert Edgington, checker. Seated from left to right: Stan Watkins, booking clerk; Mr Insall, stationmaster; and Cyril Smith, goods clerk.
Ironbridge Gorge Museum Trust

Above right:
A photograph showing how close Ironbridge & Broseley station was to the Iron Bridge itself. On Easter Monday, 30 March 1959, BR Standard Class 3, 2-6-2T No 82008, pulls away with the 1.45pm Shrewsbury-Bewdley train. *Michael Mensing*

the century they stretched for almost half a mile and were controlled from three ground frames. Both the south and middle frames were adjacent to road level crossings, the two gates of the latter wide enough to cover three tracks. By 1900 roofing tiles marked 'Broseley' were manufactured in their millions by firms such as W. P. Jones, Exley's, Prestage's and Doughty's situated between Jackfield and Broseley, and were well known in the building trade for their quality. The products of these firms were exported all over the country and

the Empire, their success in these marketplaces entirely due to the fact they could be distributed in quantity by rail along the Severn Valley line and on to the national railway network.

The railway also encouraged the opening of

Above:
Unlike the other main stations on the line, Ironbridge & Broseley station was provided with a wooden goods shed. Only a few days before closure, ex-LMS 2-6-2T No 41209 stops at the station with a southbound train, on 24 August 1963. *Andrew Muckley*

Above:
Ex-LMS 2-6-2T No 41209 disappears with its train towards Jackfield on the same day. *Andrew Muckley*

Left:
Ex-GWR 2-6-0 No 5333 shedded at Kidderminster (85D) approaches the site of Jackfield Sidings with a southbound coal train in the mid-1950s. In the background is the settlement of Madeley Wood just to the east of Ironbridge.
R. K. Blencowe

new factories to produce decorative floor and wall tiles. After travelling through Jackfield on the Severn Valley line in 1865, Yorkshire businessman Henry Dunnill declared the area '...a neglected and forlorn place...not all the world but a very poor bit of the fag end of it...'. Despite this, he obviously saw potential in establishing a rail-connected factory there, and between 1871 and 1874 he erected a purpose-built and architect-designed encaustic and decorative tileworks. His Craven Dunnill works immediately created a national and international reputation for itself, securing prestigious contracts all over the world. Even in the 1930s when trade was hard for local manufacturers and foreign contracts were no longer guaranteed, the firm was still fully occupied making and fitting tiles and other

Right:
Jackfield Sidings photographed at the beginning of the 20th century from the opposite side of the river just visible in the foreground. The chimneys are those of W. P. Jones Tileries, and to the left, the crossing keeper's cottage next to the middle ground frame. *Ron Miles Collection*

Below:
The crossing cottages along the Severn Valley line, like this one next to the middle ground frame of Jackfield Sidings, were all built to a standard design. The crossing gates here had to be large enough to span three tracks. This photograph was taken shortly after the track had been lifted.
Ironbridge Gorge Museum Trust

architectural mouldings into shops, pubs and all manner of public buildings including the GWR stations at Bristol, Reading, Haverfordwest, and the SR station at Raynes Park. (The remains of the factory survive as the Jackfield Tile Museum, part of the Ironbridge Gorge Museums.)

Not to be outdone the decorative tile makers Maw & Co soon moved from its cramped site near Ironbridge station into another purpose-built factory only a quarter of a mile to the east of Craven Dunnill. When opened in 1883 the new Benthall Works was the largest tileworks in the world employing nearly 400 people and producing 20 million tiles per annum, as well as architectural

The Severn Valley line was crucial to the viability of Maw & Co's large 1883 works seen in the foreground of this photograph taken on 27 June 1948. In the middle distance is Craven Dunnill's encaustic and decorative tileworks. The destructive landslip of 1952 occurred in the short stretch of line between the two factories. *Cambridge University Collection of Air Photographs (AV34)*

Jackfield Halt (26 miles)

Despite all this industry and a population of just over 1,000 at the end of the 19th century, Jackfield was never provided with a permanent station, only a wooden 'halt' opened on 3 December 1934. Although the industrial importance of the area had declined by then, the potential for passengers here was far greater than at any other halt on the Severn Valley line. Unfortunately, the halt was situated on top of the Doughty Fault and the unstable ground had caused problems throughout the line's history — in the worst landslip to befall Jackfield in the spring of 1952, the line and halt moved 25ft towards the river. So newsworthy was the event, that an article with photographs of the slip appeared in the Picture Post of 26 April 1952. The line was reinstated with a severe speed restriction, and a new halt was built a quarter of a mile further east and opened on 1 March 1954. It survived until the last passenger train passed over the line in September 1963.

Above:
Jackfield Halt in its original 1934 location next to the distant signal protecting the level crossing at Jackfield South Ground Frame opposite Craven Dunnill's factory out of sight in the background. The finial on top of the signal post incorporates a wheel so that the signal lamp could be lowered for refilling and then winched back into position.
Locomotive & General Railway Publishing (26910)

Below:
The 'new' 1954 Jackfield Halt with a Shrewsbury-Hartlebury service approaching in August 1963.
Andrew Muckley

Coalport (25 miles)

Like Ironbridge, this station was inconveniently situated on the opposite side of the river from the settlement, the name of which it carried. High above Coalport bridge over the river, it was within sight of the LNWR station on the north bank at the end of that company's single line branch opened on 17 June 1861 from Hadley Junction just northeast of Wellington. The river gorge was not so intensely industrialised at this point, and when first opened both stations were almost half a mile from the nearest factory, the famous Coalport China Works of John Rose & Co to the west. It was the LNWR which provided siding accommodation for this firm, and it is unlikely that the GWR received any substantial traffic to and from the works. It is perhaps significant that Coalport was the last station on the Severn Valley branch to be 'modernised' at the end of the 19th century when a second platform with loop line controlled from a fully interlocked signalbox opened at the end of 1895.

The signalbox also controlled entry into a long siding running southeast approximately half a mile to Exley & Sons Gitchfield clay mine that had been sunk in 1891. Three years later the firm opened a large roofing tile factory on the site — the Coalport Tileries — with all the very latest machinery. This factory owed its existence entirely to the railway. It was calculated that the eight kilns at the works were able to produce 250,000 tiles a week, incoming coal to fire the kilns and all this prodigious output being handled by the railway.

Exley's was already a well-established local firm, and had both supplied the bricks and built the Craven Dunnill factory at Jackfield at the beginning of the 1870s. As with this tile-making firm and Maw & Co, Exley's had to negotiate with the GWR for the rights to extract minerals from beneath the railway. In this case the firm agreed to leave coal and clay

Below:
A beautifully manicured Coalport station photographed from the road bridge looking east on 9 August 1932. On the up platform behind the platform trolley is the hut protecting the ground frame for operating the loop points behind the photographer.
Locomotive & General Railway Publishing (11808)

under the line and for a distance of 30yd (27.4m) either side over an eight-acre (3.25 hectares) area. Negotiations could be a cause of friction with the railway, as Maw & Co discovered in 1904. This firm used Arthur Grove of Bilston as its Mining Engineer, and after approaching the railway in December 1903 he reported in a handwritten letter to Maw's Board Meeting in March 1904, '…I have not heard a word from their [the GWR's] engineers and I don't suppose I shall now until we do them serious damage when they will see their folly in not coming to an accommodation with us'. Fortunately agreement was reached before Maw's mining activities threatened track stability!

Left:
William Charles Weyman, photographed at the end of his career. He was born on 11 February 1857 and joined the railway as a porter at Rhymney Junction when he turned 19. In July 1878 he was promoted to policeman at Tredegar Junction, in May 1881 became a switchman at Andoversford and then moved to Norton Junction in December 1888 to become a booking porter. He remained there to become station inspector in June 1890, and then stationmaster in November 1897. His final move was to Coalport where he took up the position of stationmaster at the age of 42 in October 1899 at the salary of 30s (£1.50) a week. It is not known exactly when he retired, but it was probably in 1923. *Ironbridge Gorge Museum Trust*

Below:
The last signalbox diagram in use at Coalport dated 5 April 1945. *Ironbridge Gorge Museum Trust*

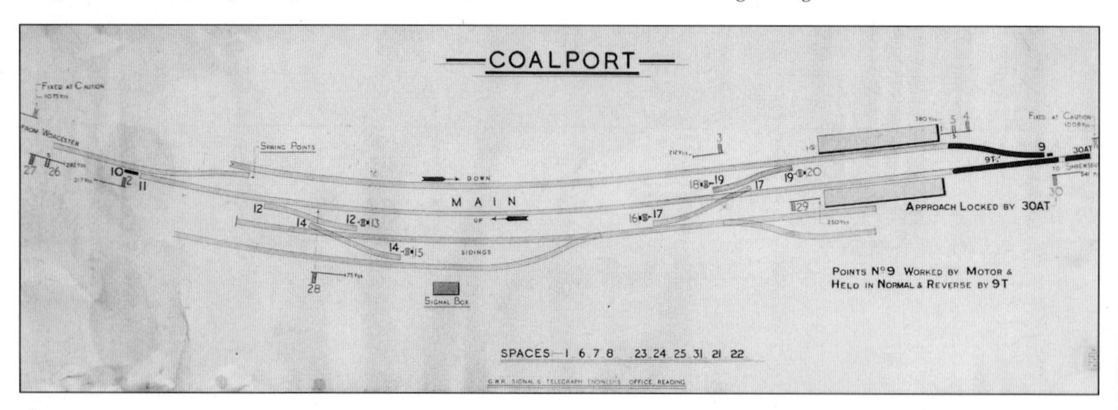

ceramics and art pottery. Unlike Craven Dunnill which used the facilities at Jackfield Sidings, Maw & Co had its own private siding controlled from a diminutive signalbox as well as its own privately owned railway wagons. All the factory's prodigious output was loaded into wagons at Jackfield and transported away along the Severn Valley line on the first leg of its journey to all parts of the Empire. The tiles which still grace the floors of the Maharaja's Palace at Mysore, India, started their journey in barrels from the sidings at Jackfield as did those for St Paul's Cathedral, Melbourne; the Women's Lunatic Asylum, Buenos Aires; the Bank of South Africa, Johannesburg; St Enoch's Station Hotel, Glasgow; the Post Office in Bombay and the Convent of St Camillus, Kilkenny, to name but a few of the locations.

Prestigious contracts such as these were hard to secure after World War 1 but, nevertheless, the siding remained comparatively busy. In the GWR's Working Timetable of October 1922, it was the down Hartlebury goods train arriving at 4.13pm, and the up 10.15am Shrewsbury goods arriving at 3.45pm which served the Maw sidings, both trains given considerable time to marshal the wagons collected there in either the yard at Ironbridge or Buildwas Junction stations. Maw & Co's sidings were one of the last to remain open in this area, finally being deleted from the Railway Clearing House Handbook of Stations in December 1959.

Above left:
The south ground frame hut immediately outside Craven Dunnill's tile factory photographed just after the line closed.
P. D. France

Below:
Although this image is not of the best quality, having been reproduced from a newspaper, it is historically too interesting to ignore. It shows Maw & Co's brand-new decorative tileworks shortly after it opened in 1883 with the signalbox which controlled entry to the private siding protected by standard McKenzie & Holland slotted post semaphore signals.
Tony Herbert Collection

Above:
Linley station sometime in the opening decade of the 20th century. The station inspector (master) here in 1886 was Edwin Lane who had started his railway career as a porter at Stourport in 1877. From Stourport he quickly moved on to Hartlebury, and then became a signalman at Bewdley in June 1878. The following year he moved to Churchill as a signalman and then in 1887 took promotion to become the station inspector at Cressage. In 1894 he moved to Wellington station and then on 7 January 1901 was made Chief Inspector at Chester station earning 50s (£2.50) a week, twice his salary when at Linley.
Ironbridge Gorge Museum Trust

Linley (22 miles)

The stretch of line between Coalport and Bridgnorth was a very scenic section but it caused the Severn Valley Railway surveyors in the 1850s more problems than anywhere else. This was not due to engineering difficulties, but protracted negotiations with Thomas C. Whitmore of Apley Park, the estate opposite the railway to the east of the River Severn. His opposition to the Severn Valley Railway plans of 1852 had forced the company to promise to run the line through tunnels to prevent it '…utterly annihilating the privacy and seclusion of the said mansion, house, park and grounds…'. This was despite the fact his property was on the opposite side of the river to the proposed railway. Raising extra capital for the construction of these tunnels helped postpone construction of the whole railway. Further negotiations with Whitmore in 1855 led to agreement for the tunnel plans to be abandoned but the price for this was high. Whitmore claimed £14,000 as compensation as well as a charge of £150 per acre for any land the railway company had to purchase from him. And in addition, he had the company agree to build a station at which at least two ordinary passenger trains in each direction every day could be stopped on request. Linley station was the result.

Bridgnorth (18 miles)

Whitmore also caused the railway company problems at Bridgnorth. For the railway enthusiast and thousands of Midlands families, Bridgnorth today is so firmly perceived as the northern terminus of the preserved Severn Valley Railway, that the impressive engineering feature which at the beginning of the 1860s got the railway from north of the town to the station to the south is completely overlooked. Bridgnorth is one of the few places in the country to have a railway tunnel immediately below the mediaeval heart of the town. To be more accurate, the tunnel, 550yd (503m) long, runs below High Town, the main settlement perched on the sandstone ledge to the west of the river. The narrow ground immediately below the cliff had, by the 1860s, wharves onto the riverside crowded with warehouses and cottages. There was simply insufficient room to drive a railway through this area and so the engineers had only two choices — to tunnel under High Town, or to

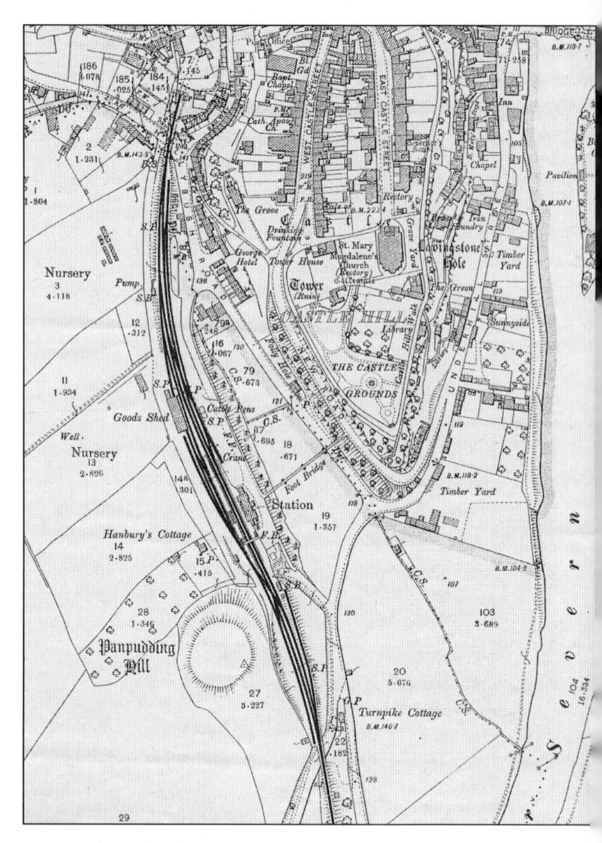

Above:
Bridgnorth, 1903.
Crown Copyright

Left:
On 30 August 1962, ex-GWR 2-6-2T No 4129 is seen heading a coal train to Ironbridge Power Station just a mile north of Bridgnorth station. The building across the river is Fort Pendlestone.
Michael Mensing

Above right:
Bridgnorth photographed in March 1962. In the foreground is the north end of the tunnel under the town, and in the background the station.
Aerofilms (A91281)

cross the river north of Bridgnorth and run through Low Town to the east putting any station inconveniently on the 'wrong' side of the river, as at Ironbridge. The plans for a railway along the Severn Valley surveyed in 1846 included a tunnel beneath High Town, but when the next plans were drawn up in 1852 by Robert Nicholson, he chose to take the line across the river at Bridgnorth and avoid Stephenson and Swanwick's tunnel. Although these plans formed part of the first successful Severn Valley Railway Act of August 1853 and its successor of July 1855, the two bridges over the river and the siting of a station east of the Severn were finally abandoned in favour of the original alignment and tunnel, given Parliamentary sanction in the Severn Valley Act of July 1856.

Although the Mayor of Bridgnorth and other 'influential inhabitants' supported this change of plan, Whitmore still had cause for dispute. He owned much of the land above the tunnel and insisted that the railway pay for that land at the prices agreed in 1855. The dispute led to litigation in Chancery in 1861, only months before the railway opened and barely four years before Whitmore's death on 13 March 1865, which finally settled matters.

When the railway arrived at Bridgnorth, the population of the town numbered 5,727, the highest of any town on the railway. In the previous 100 years, its importance as a market town had been enhanced by its position on the navigable River Severn and much of the town's prosperity and population growth in the previous century had been due to the facilities and services (warehouses, pubs, shops, boat repairers, blacksmiths, etc) it provided for the numerous barge owners who sailed along the River Severn. Within 30 years the railway had killed this river-borne traffic and because of the railway's method of freight carrying it also

Right:
The main station entrance as it appeared in the 1950s. *K. P. Lawrence*

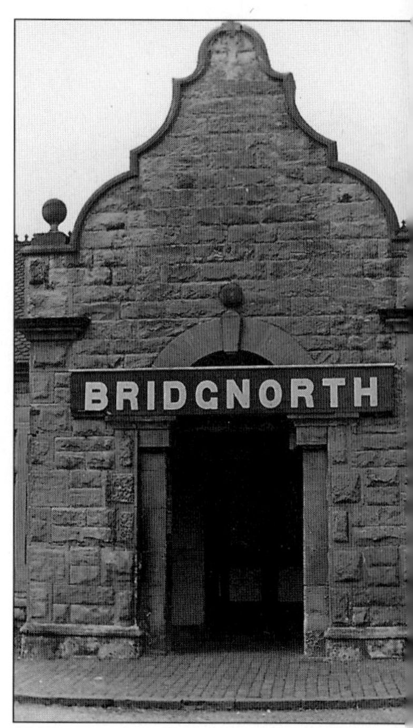

Above:
Bridgnorth station as seen from the castle either just before or just after World War 1. Between the station building and the south signalbox on the left is the corrugated tin shed used for garaging one of the buses on the Wolverhampton service.
Ironbridge Gorge Museum Trust

Below:
Bridgnorth station and the south signalbox photographed from Pan Pudding Hill in the first decade of the 20th century. *Lens of Sutton*

suffocated the river's old support infrastructures. Without the Severn Valley Railway the economy of Bridgnorth would have stagnated completely, the town losing out to other rail-connected centres. But compared to the wealth the River Severn had brought to the town in the 18th century, the Severn Valley line never benefited Bridgnorth to anything like the same extent.

If proof were needed of this, the facilities provided by the GWR at Bridgnorth altered little over the years. The stone goods shed and the station buildings themselves remained unchanged for 101 years. In 1887 the original down platform was extended, a passenger shelter erected and a cast-iron and wrought-iron lattice footbridge built to connect it to the up platform. Extra sidings were laid over the years but there were few fundamental changes to the track layout. In October 1892 two fully interlocked signalboxes were opened at the north and south ends of the station, forced on the company by the 1889 Regulation of Railways Act. After the Board of Trade's 'Requirements' had relaxed the distance facing points could be from their controlling signalbox, these were superseded in 1923 by a single central box on the up platform which remained in use until the line closed in 1963.

If the GWR was reluctant to invest too much at Bridgnorth, then the local authorities were more enthusiastic. Undoubtedly the 'influential

Right:
An official GWR photograph taken in 1925 of the coal drops at Bridgnorth station. There were eight shoots and six of the cast-iron beams used to support the rails were clearly marked 'Brymbo 1861'. Similar beams cast by this Welsh foundry were used for a number of bridges along the route of the Severn Valley line. *National Railway Museum (GWR B-Box 131/1)*

Left:
One of the GWR's petrol engined Milnes-Daimler buses which began running between Bridgnorth and Wolverhampton (Low Level) stations on 1 April 1905.
David Postle Collection

Right:
Ex-GWR railcar No W24W waiting to leave Bridgnorth for Kidderminster on 30 August 1962. This vehicle was one of 13 built for the company in 1940.
Michael Mensing

Below :
The late evening sun catches ex-LMS 2-6-2T No 41209 as it waits in the up platform at Bridgnorth with the 7.27pm to Shrewsbury on 8 June 1963. The reason it is in the 'wrong' platform for a northbound train is because it had just worked in as the 5.30pm from Shrewsbury.
Michael Mensing

Below:
Ex-GWR 2-6-2T No 4114 pulls away from Bridgnorth with a southbound mixed goods train at 3.47pm on 30 August 1962. In the adjacent siding are two horseboxes.
Michael Mensing

inhabitants' of Bridgnorth who supported the Severn Valley Railway Bill of 1856 also influenced the choice of a completely different design of station building to all the others on the line. At Bridgnorth, instead of brick as used in the simple Italianate station buildings elsewhere, stone was used and the architectural style was a restrained Jacobean. In 1887 the town corporation paid for a new approach road to the station and later, in 1895, to shorten the route from High Town to the railway, an impressive lattice footbridge was constructed at a cost of £1,400. From directly opposite the main passenger entrance to the station, the bridge leapt over Hollybush Road to reach New Road just below the remains of the castle. Ten years later in January 1905, Edward Morall, JP of Bridgnorth, visited the GWR's offices at Paddington to ask for the town to be placed on the list of stations issuing Tourist Tickets and in May that year the railway company confirmed that this had been done. Similar tickets were made available to and from Much Wenlock, Arley, Bewdley and Stourport to all parts of the country.

Above:
On the last day of through passenger services on the Severn Valley line there are more passengers than usual using the 2.20pm from Shrewsbury to Hartlebury. In conversation with the driver, the signalman rests on his shoulder the Webb & Thompson Electric Train Staff for the section between Coalport and Bridgnorth. Brought into use at Coalport on 22 October 1893, by 1963 it was only this section of line and that between Berrington and Cressage that still used staff working, all other sections being controlled by Electric Train (Key) Tokens.
Russell Mulford

This sort of innovation was a feature of the Edwardian railway scene and, even if the GWR did not want to spend money on Bridgnorth station, it was prepared to make a bold move by establishing a Bridgnorth-Wolverhampton passenger service by road. The omnibus service began on 7 November 1904 using three Clarkson steambuses but they soon proved inadequate to their task and were replaced by petrol-engined Milnes-Daimler buses from 1 April 1905. The GWR continued to run the service until 2 June 1923 when it

Above:
Ex-GWR 2-6-2T No 6128 shunts in the yard at Bridgnorth in the early 1960s. The brick building on the left behind the plate-layer's trolley was part of Bridgnorth South signalbox, built in 1892 and closed in 1923. *J. H. Moss*

was taken over by Wolverhampton Corporation.

The bus service was a response to a number of failed attempts to construct a direct railway line between Bridgnorth and Wolverhampton. The first plan had been proposed as early as 1860. The following year an attempt was made to promote a line between Bridgnorth and Dudley in the heart of the Black Country and then another line to join both the Shrewsbury & Birmingham and the Grand Junction railways near Wolverhampton was floated in 1862. The first successful Bill to receive the Royal Assent was the Bridgnorth, Wolverhampton & Staffordshire Railway authorised in June 1866 but nothing came of this project. Another attempt was made in 1872, then another in 1896 under the Government's new Light Railway Act of that year and finally at the end of 1904 the GWR

Above left:
Bridgnorth station on 24 August 1963 with a train waiting to depart for Shrewsbury. The weeds have started to appear. *Andrew Muckley*

Above:
On the same day in the opposite platform a BR diesel railcar waits to take passengers in the opposite direction, to Bewdley and on to Hartlebury.
Andrew Muckley

deposited its own plans which successfully formed part of the GWR's Additional Powers Act of July 1905. These plans were modified in 1908 so that any new line from Bridgnorth only ran as far as Wombourn, five miles southwest of Wolverhampton. There a junction was to be formed with another planned new line running north to Oxley on the Wolverhampton-Shrewsbury main line and south to the existing short branch from Kingswinford Junction. Unfortunately, by rail, Wombourn was to be a seven-mile train journey away from Wolverhampton, and this made the Bridgnorth 'extension' look very unattractive. The line between Oxley Junction and the Kingswinford branch via Wombourn was opened to passengers on 11 May 1925, and although the GWR renewed its powers for the Bridgnorth extension two years later, this part of the project never materialised.

For the next few miles out of Bridgnorth, the Severn Valley line lost sight of the river. A mile south of the station, a loop capable of accommodating 35 standard wagons, plus engine and brake van, was opened at the end of August 1922 to serve a local brickworks. Knowle Sand Brick Works Siding was provided with ground frames at either end of the loop, unlocked by a key in the end of the Electric Train Staff. The 1922 Working Timetable records that if the 8.15am Shrewsbury to Kidderminster goods had 'traffic' for the siding, the signalman at Bridgnorth had to telephone his colleague at Highley signalbox, the reverse of the procedure if the 8.40am Hartlebury-Shrewsbury goods had reason to enter the loop.

Eardington (16 miles)

Eardington was not one of the GWR's interwar 'halts' but appeared in timetables soon after the railway had opened. The single platform was provided for workers at the nearby Upper and Lower Forges connected by a 750yd (686m)-long canal tunnel which ran under the railway. The Lower Forge next to the river dated back to the late 1770s, whilst the Upper Forge on the Mor Brook to the west was of a slightly later date. The production of charcoal wrought-iron continued until the end of the 1880s, after which the works almost certainly closed although there is conflicting evidence as to the date of final abandonment.

Between the crossing of Mor Brook half a mile south of Eardington and Hampton Loade station, the railway once again shadowed the river to the east. In fact, all the way to Arley, some seven miles, the railway and river were never more than a few hundred metres apart.

Left:
Eardington station covered with enamel advertising signs in the first decade of the 20th century. It might be expected that this remote station did very little trade, but statistics show that 5,944 tickets were issued in 1903. Ten years later the total soared to 6,690, beating the number of tickets issued at Coalport by 68!
Lens of Sutton

Below:
Eardington remained opened until the passenger service north of Bewdley was withdrawn in 1963, and this was its appearance in that final year.
Andrew Muckley

Hampton Loade (13½ miles)

Interestingly, in Kelly's 19th century directories, Hampton Loade station is mentioned only in passing under the Chelmarsh village heading. Chelmarsh village was a good two miles to the west of the river and the station, and the hamlet of Hampton Loade itself was on the east of the river, a ferry journey away from the station. Originally there was just one platform, but another was added in 1882 next to a new loop enabling trains to be crossed at the station. A new fully interlocked signalbox was opened at the same time.

Leaving Hampton Loade and travelling south, the line entered what became the Wyre Forest Coalfield. Approaching Highley from

Left:
Hampton Loade signalbox, built in 1882/3 by McKenzie & Holland, the signalling contractors of Worcester. The firm used the timber version of its standard design here, but for the signalboxes built at the same time at Highley and Arley, brick bases with wooden superstructures were used.
J. H. Moss

Below:
The fireman of ex-GWR 0-6-0 pannier tank No 8714 prepares to surrender the Bridgnorth-Hampton Loade electric train (key) token to the signalman at Hampton Loade in April 1954. *Real Photographs*

the north were the sidings serving Alveley Colliery opened to the east of the river and the railway in 1935, the last colliery developed in this area. According to official railway notices, the sidings capable of holding 85 wagons and the coal screens were brought into use on 30 January 1939, the north and south ground frames released by Electric Train (Key) Token. Coal was transported to the sidings and coal screens in narrow gauge wheeled tubs attached to a continuous cable, the track crossing the river on a new concrete bridge. Alveley Colliery was one of those interwar industrial developments — including the opening of the sugarbeet factory at Kidderminster in 1925 and the building of Buildwas electricity generating station in 1932 — that appeared to offer the Severn Valley line a new lease of life. Coal from Alveley did eventually keep the southern section of the line open after the rest had closed in 1963, but the renaissance was short-lived as the mine closed in January 1969.

Left:
Photographed in June 1967 four years after closure, Hampton Loade station building had remained unaltered since it opened in 1862. The waiting room had never been extended as at Berrington, Highley and Arley, and no extra bedroom had been added either. *Andrew Muckley*

Below:
Alveley Colliery's coal screens and sidings photographed on 9 February 1939 only 10 days after they had been officially brought into use. The line nearest the camera is the Severn Valley line running towards Highley to the right and Hampton Loade to the left. Just north of Highley a single platform was constructed for the use of miners working at Alveley Colliery. *National Railway Museum (GWR B Box 326/17)*

Highley (11 miles)

The population of Highley when the railway arrived was just 407, so the work of the first stationmaster, Samuel Edwards, could not have been too demanding. The station buildings were to the same standard design as elsewhere on the line but constructed not of brick but of stone, probably quarried locally. As with the other village stations on the Severn Valley line, Highley catered for a predominantly local

Top right:
Ex-LMS 2-6-2T No 40110 enters Highley station on 5 March 1960 with a train from Shrewsbury. *David Postle Collection*

Above:
Highley station and yard on 24 June 1967 during the period when coal trains were still running to Alveley Colliery sidings. *Andrew Muckley*

Right:
Rowland Lucas was the only remaining member of staff at Highley when this photograph was taken from a special on 2 March 1968. He became signalman at the station after the regular passenger service had been withdrawn having been a miner at Highley mine and later Alveley colliery. He was made redundant in February 1969. *Andrew Muckley*

Right:
0-6-0 saddle tank built for the Highley Mining Co by Andrew Barclay of Kilmarnock in 1896 and christened *Kinlet*. It could only have been a few months, or perhaps weeks, old when this photograph was taken. *Mrs Viggars*

Above:
A good overall view of the surface buildings of Highley pit in the 1920s. Underground work must have been advancing well judging by the quantity of timber pit-props in the yard.
David Postle Collection

Right:
The Gloucester Railway Carriage & Wagon Co's official photograph taken in 1923 of another 10-ton wagon for the Highley Mining Co.
National Railway Museum

farming community who might travel to and from Bridgnorth or Bewdley or occasionally further afield. A cattle dock was provided at the station at the beginning of 1870. However, at the end of the 1870s, coal-mining began to change the landscape in this part of Shropshire and by World War 1 Highley was a completely different place. The construction of red-brick houses and rows of terraces was followed by a Co-operative Store, a Working Men's Club in 1905 and a Methodist Chapel in 1913. By 1921 the population of Highley had risen to 1,985, at least 500 men working at Highley pit. This growth in the local population meant Highley's passenger traffic remained healthy even between the world wars when at other stations passenger numbers were declining rapidly. The number of tickets issued at Highley averaged 22,000 a year in the 1930s, higher than at Bridgnorth or Stourport, and was comparable with sales at Ironbridge.

The coal boom started in the 1870s with the reopening of Billingsley pit a few miles to the west of Highley. It had originally gone into production in 1796, coal travelling down to the River Severn along a cast-iron plateway. Two blast furnaces were constructed next to the colliery, but these and the pit were abandoned in the first decade of the 19th century. Shortly after Billingsley was reopened, a completely new pit was sunk just to the west of Highley station in 1879, and then in 1892 the Highley Mining Company started work on Kinlet Colliery to the south. Rail connections were provided to all three collieries. In fact, it is very unlikely that there would have been a revival of coal-mining without the presence of the Severn Valley line. The connection to Highley mine left the yard immediately south of the station, wagons then being hauled up a

Right:
The 10.10am Hartlebury-Coton Hill (Shrewsbury) goods approaching Highley at 12.10pm on 24 September 1955. Out of sight in the foreground is the connection to Highley Colliery.
F. W. Shuttleworth

rope-worked incline to the colliery. In 1882, accompanying the necessary alterations to the yard at Highley station, McKenzie & Holland of Worcester erected and equipped a fully interlocked signalbox. The connections to Kinlet and Billingsley mines were a mile further south. A siding was laid on the west side of the line south of the viaduct over Borle Brook and a connection made from there along the brook to Kinlet mine according to an agreement between the GWR and the Highley Mining Co of May 1895. Further sidings adjacent to the Severn Valley line were added a few years later.

Kinlet sidings had originally formed part of an agreement of August 1878 with the Billingsley Colliery Co for a link to its new pit but this had been allowed to lapse. It was not until just before World War 1 that another single track line was pushed further along the

Left:
On 25 June 1960, ex-GWR diesel railcar No 26 crosses the Borle Brook just south of Highley with a service to Bewdley. The vehicle is just about to pass the site of Kinlet & Billingsley signalbox and the sidings at the foot of the branches to those two collieries.
Michael Mensing

Left;
The sidings and coal screens at the foot of the incline (just visible on the left) from Billingsley colliery. This early 20th century view was taken looking east in the direction from which the branch came in from the Severn Valley line. The two 10-ton wagons in the centre of the photograph were owned by the tile makers Maw & Co, Jackfield. *Mrs Viggars*

Borle Brook to Billingsley Colliery, a trek of four miles. The quantity of coal then reaching the Severn Valley line was such that Kinlet sidings had to be extended again and in December 1913 a fully interlocked signalbox was opened to replace the ground frames. All this extra traffic also forced the GWR to erect a lattice footbridge at the south end of Highley station at the same time, the accommodation crossing linking the station's single platform to the road to and from the village, frequently obstructed by stationary coal trains.

Both Highley and Billingsley collieries ran their own steam locomotives. Andrew Barclay 0-6-0 saddle tank No 782 ran at Kinlet from new in 1896 until the 1920s. It was replaced by a secondhand Hunslet 0-4-0 saddle tank, and joined in 1933 by a similar Hudswell Clarke locomotive, No 1401. But coal mining in this part of Shropshire was comparatively short-lived. Billingsley Colliery was the first to close in 1922, followed by Kinlet in 1935. By this time the workings of Highley mine had run under the river, and during the 1930s a brand new colliery — Alveley — was developed on the east side of the Severn to exploit the seams there. After 1940 all coal was brought up at Alveley, this arrangement lasting until both mines closed permanently in the winter of 1968-9. Kinlet signalbox closed in 1943 and the sidings were finally taken out of use in June 1964.

Arley (9 miles)

Two miles from Highley, Arley station was situated on a gentle curve with the station buildings on the east of the line high above the river. The village of Arley (or more accurately Upper Arley) was within sight of the station at the same altitude but it was a ferry journey away on the other side of the river. As with the other village stations on the line originally it was not possible to cross trains there, the loop, second platform and signalbox not brought into use until 1883. Minor alterations were carried out in the years before World War 1, but after that and until closure, Arley remained an unspoiled and tranquil station. Its idyllic situation prompted the GWR to write in its publication 'Handy Aids' series No 7 — *The Severn Valley* (1913 and 1923): 'At Arley, where there is an abundance of good accommodation, the holiday-maker will find himself in the midst of echoing woods,

Right:
Arley station c1908 looking from the road overbridge in the direction of Highley. This photograph is a very rare illustration of a goods train on the Severn Valley line in its best years just before World War 1. We must be grateful to Mr White the photographer. *Lens of Sutton*

Below:
A northbound late afternoon passenger train at Arley on 7 September 1932 hauled by GWR 4-4-0 No 3557. *Selwyn Pearce Higgins (Q167), National Railway Museum*

verdant meadows, stately trees, fruitful orchards, rich cornfields, and picturesque hedgerows. Here he sees the "Silver Severn" at its best...'. At Arley, the loss of local goods traffic in the 1930s was actually turned to advantage when in 1938 one of the station-sidings provided the space for the GWR's second Camping Coach on the Severn Valley line (the other was at Hampton Loade).

Running southwards from the station in two broad reverse curves, the line then crossed the River Severn into Worcestershire on the impressive Victoria Bridge. Clinging then to the eastern banks of the river, the railway headed towards the riverside town of Bewdley. Between 1899 and 1906, approximately a mile and a quarter from Arley, there was a siding for the use of the contractors constructing the section of the Elan Valley Aqueduct, bringing water to the city of Birmingham. The pipes ran under the railway and crossed the river at this point on another impressive iron bridge, photographs of which were sold as postcards.

Left:
During the summer of 1962, signalwoman Mrs Jones exchanges tokens with the fireman of ex-GWR 2-6-2T No 4175 heading a down freight through Arley. *B. S. Moone*

Below:
On another shift in the same year, Fred Jones prepares to pass the Arley-Highley token to the fireman of ex-GWR 2-6-2T No 5153 entering the station with a northbound freight. Mr and Mrs Jones worked at Arley as porter-signalmen from the 1930s until the signalbox closed on 28 June 1964, living in the station house until their deaths in the early 1970s. *B. S. Moone*

Above:
Arley station shortly before it was closed to passengers by British Railways in September 1963. *Andrew Muckley*

Below:
The GWR's official postcard of Victoria Bridge, Arley. *David Postle Collection*

Northwood Halt (7 miles)

A few hundred metres further south and halfway between Arley and Bewdley stations, the GWR built another of its interwar halts — Northwood Halt — opened on 17 June 1935. This single platform served the growing scatter of holiday bungalows on this stretch of the river, little holiday retreats as British as deckchairs and beachside chalets.

Half a mile from Northwood Halt, the single line from Tenbury approached from the west across the river, and then paralleled the Severn Valley line all the way into Bewdley station. The Tenbury & Bewdley Railway was opened to regular passenger traffic on 13 August 1864 as a continuation of the Tenbury Railway which had opened a few years earlier on 1 August 1861 from Woofferton Junction on the Shrewsbury-Hereford main line. It is interesting to note that to control the junction of the Tenbury & Bewdley line and the Severn Valley branch at Bewdley, the Worcester firm McKenzie, Clunes & Holland (later McKenzie & Holland) was awarded the contract to erect semaphore signals and a signalbox fitted with a 'Chambers Patent Junction Signal Apparatus'. This type of lever frame was one of the first fully interlocked lever frame designs on the market, having been patented in 1860, and at this time was still a viable rival to Stevens & Sons and John Saxby's equipment that had appeared in the same year. Bewdley signalbox just south of the station buildings was, consequently, the first recognisable signalbox on the Severn Valley line.

Below
Northwood Halt on 25 August 1963 with a train approaching from Bewdley. *Andrew Muckley*

Bewdley (5½ miles)

At Bridgnorth the railway ultimately depressed the economy of the town but at Bewdley a depression had already set in when the Severn Valley line opened. The predominant architecture of the riverside and town centre remains today solidly 18th-century Georgian, indicating in a very tangible way when the town stopped developing.

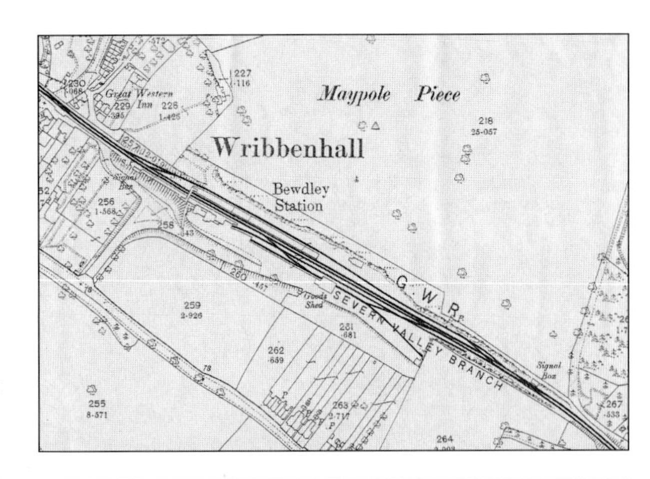

Top right:
Bewdley, 1903.
Crown Copyright

Above:
BR Standard Class 3 2-6-2T No 82004 runs alongside the Bewdley & Tenbury Railway line just under a mile from Bewdley. The train is the 1.45pm from Shrewsbury photographed on 20 June 1959.
Michael Mensing

Right:
Two months later in the same location, the same train is headed by ex-GWR 0-6-0 pannier tank No 3769.
Michael Mensing

The wealth and importance of Bewdley had been dependent on its position as an inland port on the River Severn, on the early 18th century's main 'motorway' between the Midlands, Gloucester and Bristol. An observer in 1756 counted 313 'barges' (some up to 60ft long) plying between Shrewsbury and Bewdley. When the Staffordshire &

Left:
Wribbenhall Viaduct at the north end of Bewdley station photographed in October 1966. The standard GWR lower quadrant signals on the impressive timber post controlled entry to either side of the up island platform. The post and arms were moved by the preservation society and re-erected at Arley in 1976. *Selwyn Pearce Higgins (1966/161), National Railway Museum*

Above:
Edwardian Bewdley station looking northwest. *David Postle Collection*

Right:
Standing proudly to the right of this oak from the Wyre Forest in the yard at Bewdley is stationmaster, Ernest James Neale Carter. He joined the GWR in 1894 in the Rates Department at Gloucester, and became stationmaster at Bewdley on 26 August 1914, staying until 10 November 1927.
David Postle Collection

Worcestershire Canal opened in 1771 bypassing the town to join the river three miles further downstream where the River Stour flowed into the Severn, Bewdley's river traffic was affected and with it the wealth of the town. Where the canal joined the river next to the River Stour a new port was created — Stourport. Bewdley did not decline immediately, but the wealth

Above right:
Bewdley station c1908-11 with one of the LNWR's through carriages which ran between Birmingham and Woofferton Junction. In the opposite platform is a GWR rail-motor. *Lens of Sutton*

Right:
The driver of this Thornycroft lorry demonstrates the advantages of a simple lever in Bewdley station yard for an official GWR photograph of 1929. The vehicle was part of the GWR's County Lorry Service. *National Railway Museum (GWR B Box 208/10)*

Below:
Shunted into 'Rock Siding' at Bewdley, ex-GWR 2-6-2T No 4116 waits with the empty coaching stock of a LMS excursion from Walsall on 2 July 1949. *Selwyn Pearce Higgins(1949/16), National Railway Museum*

Left:
On 15 April 1963, another ex-GWR 2-6-2T, No 4140, runs into Bewdley station from the south.
B. S. Moone

Below:
At the north end of Bewdley, the signalman prepares to hand over the token to the driver of ex-GWR diesel railcar No W32W forming the 2.10pm Kidderminster-Woofferton Junction train on 24 September 1955.
F. W. Shuttleworth

that had once flowed into the town from waterborne trade ebbed away and was finally killed altogether by the Severn Valley line. When the railway arrived in the parish of Wribbenhall on the opposite side of the river to Bewdley, there were still tens of horse-drawn and sailing coal barges and trows on the river. But in 1885 the company maintaining the towpath between Coalbrookdale and Bewdley gave up its powers, and 10 years later all the commercial vessels were gone, the last having sunk on 25 January 1895 after colliding with the bridge over the river at Bridgnorth.

The original Bewdley station buildings on the down side of the line remained almost unaltered throughout their working life, as did the goods shed. The biggest changes came in the 1870s when a single-line branch was opened to Kidderminster. The 'Kidderminster loop' had been planned in 1860 when the Severn Valley Railway was under construction, an Act being secured the following year. The project was given impetus when the LNWR as joint owners of the line between Woofferton

Junction and Tenbury, foreseeing the possibility of running through trains between the West Midlands via Kidderminster and Bewdley onto the Shrewsbury and Hereford main line, negotiated in 1863 with the West Midlands and GWR companies who leased the Tenbury & Bewdley Railway. The outcome was an agreement from the latter companies to complete the Kidderminster line by 1865. But this did not happen, and even after two further Acts had been obtained in 1868 and 1872, there was still no sign of a direct Bewdley-Kidderminster link. Eventually, after the GWR had failed to persuade Parliament of the merits of a direct line between Bewdley and Stourbridge in 1873, and it seemed possible that the LNWR would finally see the fruition of its aspirations to link Woofferton Junction with the Black Country by backing the 1874 plans of the West Staffordshire Railway for a connection from the Tenbury line north of Bewdley to Wolverhampton, the GWR committed itself to building the Kidderminster loop. Work started at the very end of 1874 and the line was finally opened to traffic on 1 June 1878.

With trains then approaching Bewdley from four directions, an island platform was created, on which a neat shelter complete with an elliptical corrugated iron roof was erected, opposite the main station buildings. At either end of the improved layout new signalboxes were built — Bewdley North and Bewdley South — McKenzie & Holland winning the contract to replace its 1864 equipment.

The LNWR immediately took advantage of the Kidderminster loop when it opened, running through carriages between Woofferton Junction and Birmingham as well as a number of goods and coal trains. The 'Tenbury Goods' between Stourbridge Junction and Hereford via Bewdley and Woofferton, which started life at this time, lasted until 1949. Through carriages were discontinued at the end of World War 1, but regular passenger services between Woofferton Junction and Bewdley ran until the Tenbury-Woofferton section closed to passengers in July 1961. As an experiment between 1905 and 1916 one of the GWR's new steam railmotors was tried on some of these services but steam-hauled trains continued from then on until 1953 when they were replaced by ex-GWR streamlined diesel railcars.

Its status as a junction station meant that Bewdley issued far more tickets every year than any other station on the Severn Valley

A deserted Bewdley station photographed on 25 August 1963. *Andrew Muckley*

Above:
Mount Pleasant Tunnel photographed in April 1987. *Author*

Left:
Bewdley porter, Stan Perry, at the end of his railway career, is about to hand over paperwork to the guard of the Kidderminster-Cleobury Mortimer freight on the morning of 26 March 1965. *Andrew Muckley*

line. Ironically, the actual income generated from passengers was only on a par with Bridgnorth and Stourport, and freight receipts only brought in a fraction of what those stations generated and was well below the totals recorded for Ironbridge or even Highley, its figures boosted by coal traffic.

In the end, Bewdley's link with the Birmingham Snow Hill-Worcester main line proved more important than with stations further north on the Severn Valley line or east into rural Shropshire. The passenger service between Bewdley and Tenbury Wells was withdrawn on 29 July 1962, but after the Bewdley-Shrewsbury passenger trains stopped running in September 1963, a service between Bewdley, Kidderminster and Hartlebury was maintained. It was not until 5 January 1970 that these trains were discontinued and the line to Bewdley finally closed. The closure was, however, short-lived and reinstatement of a very different type of passenger service came on 18 May 1974, when the 'new' Severn Valley Railway ran its first fare-paying passengers into Bewdley from Bridgnorth.

One and a quarter miles south of Bewdley, the original Severn Valley line passed through Mount Pleasant tunnel (124yd [113.4m]) on its way to Hartlebury Junction. Just beyond the tunnel on 31 March 1930, the single-platform Burlish Halt was opened to serve one of Stourport's growing suburbs. A little under a year previously, a siding had been opened here for the Shropshire, Worcestershire & Staffordshire Electric Power Development Co Ltd, the owners of the electricity generating station to the southeast of Stourport. These sidings lasted until 1966 by which time they were used by Steatite & Porcelain Products Ltd whose factory, producing amongst other things high-voltage ceramic insulators, was close by. Just beyond these sidings on the approaches to Stourport station, the wartime Ministry of Food opened a large cold storage depot served by a number of sidings in December 1941.

Stourport (3 miles)

The original station building at Stourport was almost identical to that provided at Buildwas and Bewdley, and from the railways opening in February 1862 there were two platforms and a loop where trains could pass. As at all the principal stations on the Severn Valley line, Stourport was also provided with a small goods yard and goods shed. All these buildings were situated south of the railway nearest the town where the main road to Kidderminster crossed the line on the level. Although when first opened the railway was just north of the town, of all the stations on the Severn Valley line it was undoubtedly the most convenient for the population it was intended to serve.

When the Severn Valley line arrived, Stourport was almost as populous as Bewdley (3,158 and 2,958 respectively) despite having been in existence for less than a century. But Stourport's fortunes were not what they had

Below:
Stourport station on 3 January 1969 a year before it closed. The flat-roofed room to the right of the British Rail sign and the first-floor extension on the extreme right are both later additions. Without these additions, the other stations built exactly to the same configuration with two gabled buildings at right angles to the track joined by a single-storey unit were at Bewdley and Buildwas Junction. At these locations and at Stourport there were no bay windows on the platform side. At Ironbridge & Broseley station the same plan was used but the stationmaster's two-storey accommodation was not built, which meant only the smaller of the gabled units with the three-light rectangular bay window and the 'connecting' unit were constructed. At all other stations, the gabled building with the rectangular bay window, seen here on the left, was omitted and only the stationmaster's accommodation and the adjacent single-storey unit were put up. At these locations, the structure was orientated so that the three-sided bay window was on the platform side. *Andrew Muckley*

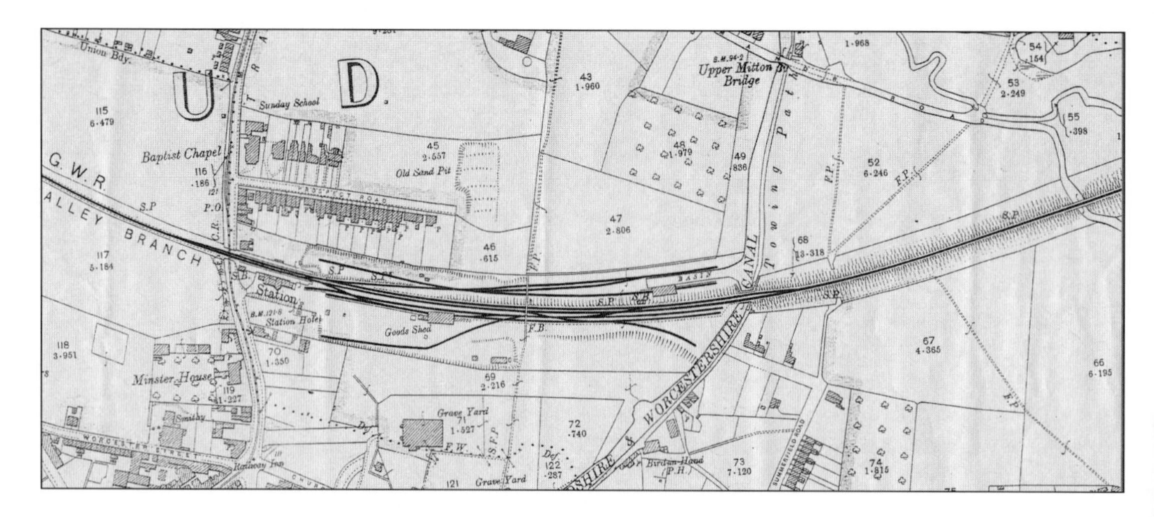

been in the prosperous years immediately following the opening of the Staffordshire & Worcestershire Canal at the beginning of the 1770s. When the Birmingham & Worcester Canal was completed in 1815, a significant tonnage of traffic that had once passed through Stourport had been diverted away to the new waterway. Within three decades of the arrival of the Severn Valley railway line, all commercial river traffic at both Bewdley and Stourport had also dried up. The Staffordshire & Worcestershire Canal, however, did continue to carry commercial traffic even into the 1930s, as the examples mentioned below will illustrate.

Top:
Stourport, 1903.
Crown Copyright

Above right and right:
In the top photograph, the driver and fireman check around ex-GWR 2-6-2T No 5153 at Stourport before it pulls away with a northbound freight (lower picture).
Lens of Sutton

At the beginning of 1885 a basin from the Staffordshire & Worcestershire Canal was opened just east of the railway station at Stourport, with new sidings laid in opposite the original goods yard. This allowed coal, iron and steel to be brought in by rail and then taken by canal to Wilden Ironworks less than a mile from the station. At the same time, the GWR took the opportunity to provide two new interlocked signalboxes either end of the layout. Even though the railway ran through Stourport station on an east-west alignment, the signalbox at the level crossing was christened the 'North Box' whilst its partner opposite the canal basin was named Stourport South. From the end of 1887, the double line between the two boxes was worked under absolute block regulations.

Left:
Stourport-on-Severn station at the end of the 1950s. Clearly visible is the extension to the north signalbox added in 1951 so that the box could accommodate a larger frame of 43 levers, allowing the south signalbox to be closed on 1 April that year.
J. H. Moss

Below:
A DMU bound for Bewdley departs from Stourport in March 1966. *Andrew Muckley*

Surprisingly, the Staffordshire & Worcestershire Canal was an important factor in the siting of the Shropshire & Worcestershire Electric Power Co's power station at Stourport after World War 1. Although sidings and a branch off the Severn Valley line were authorised in the same 1918 Act for building the power station, almost all coal was delivered by canal or river to the first boilerhouse opened in 1926, and the second one completed in 1936. It was only in May 1940 that a direct rail connection from the Severn Valley line was brought into use. The two original narrow gauge (2ft 6in [76cm]) English Electric Co'sbattery locomotives that had been used to move coal delivered by barge to the boilerhouses or stockpiles then found themselves working next to two standard gauge 0-4-0 saddle tank steam locomotives, one supplied by Andrew Barclay (No 2088 *Sir Thomas Royden*), the other purchased in 1942 from Bagnall's (No 2665 General Wade Hayes). These were joined in 1958 by another saddle tank, standard Peckett 0-4-0 No 1893, which had been sent when new in 1936 to Ironbridge power station at Buildwas Junction. By the end of the 1970s all the locomotives were redundant, and on 12 January 1981 the connection with the Severn Valley line was officially closed. The power station itself that had been a dominant riverside feature for nearly 60 years closed completely at the end of March 1984 and was demolished soon afterwards.

Between Stourport and Hartlebury Junction there were just two more private sidings, one opened during World War 1 to serve a sand quarry, the other brought into use in August 1939 for the use of the RAF during World War 2.

Below:
Stourport power station photographed soon after World War 2, its brick chimneys still prominently camouflaged! In the foreground is the River Severn, and at the top of the photograph the branch leading to the Severn Valley line. *A. J. Booth Collection*

Bewdley to Kidderminster

As described elsewhere, this part of the Severn Valley Railway opened in 1878, although it had been planned in 1860 before the main branch line was completed. The junction between the Hartlebury and Kidderminster lines was made at Bewdley South, the two single lines running parallel for a short distance before going their separate ways. Less than a mile from Bewdley the GWR opened Rifle Range Halt in June 1905, served by the railmotor service between Hartlebury, Bewdley and Kidderminster. It closed on 4 October 1920 two years after the railmotors had been withdrawn.

The line then entered Bewdley Tunnel (480yd [439m] long) which after only 30 years of use had to be relined completely between 1908 and 1910. Half a mile on the Kidderminster side of this tunnel the GWR opened Foley Park Halt on 2 January 1905, and unlike its partner at Rifle Range, its location on the main Stourport-Kidderminster road helped secure its survival until the passenger service to Bewdley was withdrawn by British Rail in 1970. By then it was on the north of the line, repositioned in 1925 to make way for new sidings into the factory of the West Midland Sugar Co Ltd.

The refining of locally grown sugarbeet was

Above:
The interior of Hartlebury Junction signalbox. The McKenzie & Holland box opened in June 1876 and the 27-lever frame shown here was installed in 1912. The box closed on 15 May 1977.
W. H. A. Thompson/
D. J. Powell Collection

Left:
Hartlebury Junction signalbox in the 1960s looking towards Kidderminster. This is where the Severn Valley branch left the former Oxford, Worcester & Wolverhampton Railway, the junction just visible in the background on the left.
W. H. A. Thompson/
D. J. Powell Collection

Left:
A number of Severn Valley branch trains departed from and terminated at Hartlebury station. In this view taken on 19 September 1959, an ex-GWR diesel railcar waits in the down platform with a Severn Valley line service. *V. R. Webster*

Above:
Foley Park Halt in its post-1925 position on the north side of the railway. Photographed in March 1966, the main Stourport to Kidderminster road crosses the line on the bridge in the background. *Andrew Muckley*

Right:
Ex-GWR 2-6-2T No 5518 emerges from Bewdley Tunnel with a train for Bewdley on 4 August 1959. *B. S. Moone*

Left:
The Kidderminster sugar beet factory of the West Midland Sugar Co photographed on 17 February 1926, barely a year after it opened. The factory was built at 45° to the Severn Valley line, on which a row of wagons can be seen in the background.
National Railway Museum (GWR B Box 159/6)

Below:
The impressive exterior of Kidderminster station as it appeared just before World War 1.
David Postle Collection

a comparatively recent innovation in this country, the first factory having opened in 1912 at Cantley in Norfolk. In 1921 the Home Grown Sugar Co set up the country's second factory just outside Newark-on-Trent on the Kelham Estate, and the organisations operating these two works and other interested parties persuaded the Government of the benefits of not having to rely on imported sugar from the colonies, especially in times of war. As a result of the Trade Facilities Acts of 1921-26, finance was then made available to build sugarbeet factories at nine other locations, one of which was just south of Kidderminster. Siting the new factories next to railways was considered essential as 93% of all beet was initially delivered by rail. But this percentage was very soon eroded and when the British Sugar Corporation was formed in 1936 to administer all the country's 18 factories, deliveries by lorry were becoming increasingly important.

Nevertheless, thousands of tons of beet continued to arrive by rail during the winter 'campaign' months and the importance of the connection from the Severn Valley line can be judged by the fact that the sidings were not taken out of use until June 1983. At the time of writing (1998) the factory is still in production though rebuilt and much larger than when it first opened.

Just beyond the sugarbeet factory, the railway crossed the River Stour and the Staffordshire & Worcestershire Canal on a seven-arched brick viaduct before turning northwards to join the former Oxford, Worcester & Wolverhampton Railway main line at Kidderminster Junction, less than half a mile from Kidderminster station.

Left:
GWR 2-4-0 waiting at the down platform at Kidderminster station in the 1890s.
Hereford & Worcester County Council, Kidderminster Library

Below:
Ex-GWR diesel railcar No W24W in the same platform at Kidderminster. The train is the 2.5pm departure for Shrewsbury photographed in May 1961. *Russell Mulford*

4. Decline and Closure

The closure of the Severn Valley line as a through route came in September 1963 almost exactly 101 years after the line had opened. Quite when the Severn Valley line ceased to be commercially viable is difficult to pinpoint. There appeared to have been few economies of operation in the last few years before closure which might have helped prolong the life of the line. But perhaps by then no reduction of facilities or alterations to the infrastructure would have been enough to save the line.

Most people believe the branch was closed because passengers were lured away to buses between the world wars and then into their own private cars in the 1950s with no attempt made to win them back to the railway. But the causes were far more complex than that, and the present author will undoubtedly surprise many readers by stating that he believes the seeds of the line's ultimate failure were sown in the 17 years between 1845 and 1862 before the line opened.

The original plans to push a double-track railway alongside the River Severn started life in 1845. If it had been constructed then and had become an established main line through route as planned, it might have survived longer than 100 years. But it opened 17 years too late as a single-track branch line with only five places on its 40½-mile length where trains could pass, its capacity for handling traffic immediately handicapped from the start.

If it had opened as a main line, its existence would have been justified in two fundamental ways: revenue would have been generated by through traffic, as well as from the stations and goods sidings on the route. As a single-track branch line, however, viability relied solely on the performance of every station and siding on the line. On the Severn Valley branch only one station served a population larger than 5,500, only three towns had close to half that number of inhabitants, and all the rest were counted in the hundreds. Neither were these settlements expanding at the rate of those industrial towns a few miles east in the Black Country, for example.

Every station (except Bridgnorth) was built to a basic standard design and provided with the same basic facilities — booking office/waiting room, public toilets, accommodation for a resident stationmaster and at least one goods siding. At some places this level of provision could be justified (Ironbridge & Broseley, Bridgnorth, Bewdley, Stourport); at other places it was questionable (Berrington, Cressage, Buildwas, Coalport, Arley), but at Linley the accommodation was extravagant. There was no road between the village of Linley (where the local population numbered only 94 when the railway arrived) and the station over a mile away. The nearest other settlement, Astley Abbotts with a population of 668, had no direct road connection to the railway either. It was true that the railway company had been coerced into providing a station by Thomas C. Whitmore of Apley Park;

Above:
Linley station in August 1963 with a train approaching from the Bridgnorth direction. *Andrew Muckley*

but he died in 1865, and yet the station remained open for another 98 years unaltered. In 1903 when 159 tons of goods traffic was dealt with at Linley, Bridgnorth four miles away was coping with 46,455 tons. By 1921 the population of Linley had dropped to 53, whilst the numbers living at Astley Abbotts had fallen to 505. Despite this it was not until September 1951 that the siding at Linley was closed and the station reduced to the status of a halt, by which time every station on the line had long since ceased to be financially viable.

The Severn Valley line also opened in 1862 without the planned branches into Coalbrookdale and up the valley adjacent to Coalport. Access to the industries and coal mines on the north side of the river in this area had been an important goal for a number of Railway Mania projects (see Chapter 1) and was vital if any line along the Severn Valley was to prosper. In 1845, the ironworks at both Coalbrookdale and Horsehay were connected by plateway to the River Severn to the south on to which they dispatched their finished products. The Shropshire Union/Severn Valley Railway branch was intended to supersede these plateways and take traffic away from the river. But not only was the branch never built, by the time the Severn Valley line opened, Coalbrookdale and Horsehay traffic was heading in the opposite direction compared to 17 years previously, and travelling northwards by rail to the Shrewsbury-Birmingham main line at Ketley Junction. In fact it was due to the considerable financial backing of the Coalbrookdale Co that the line between Lightmoor Junction, Horsehay and Ketley Junction had been opened in 1858.

When the Coalport branch was planned by the Shropshire Union Railway it must have been aware that in 1830 an impressive 80,000

Right:
A deserted Berrington station shortly before the passenger service was withdrawn. *Lens of Sutton*

Below:
Ironbridge from the air in October 1934, in the same year the Iron Bridge seen in the centre of the photograph was closed to vehicular traffic. As a result of this closure all railway deliveries to and from the town had a long detour before they could reach their destination. *Aerofilms (46398)*

tons of coal from the East Shropshire Coalfield had passed down the Shropshire Canal to Coalport where it was loaded into Severn 'trows' for transport down river. The Severn Valley Railway promoters undoubtedly hoped to capture this trade for themselves, but once again, by the time the Severn Valley line opened, this canal traffic had already been lured away from the river to the railway network opened further north in the 1840s and 1850s. The same was true of the pig-iron produced in the blast furnaces at Blists Hill only a mile north of Coalport. In the 1840s the supporters of a railway along the Severn valley, conscious of the success of this new ironworks, intended to serve this site from their own line. But by 1862 Blists Hill's output of pig iron was also travelling northwards away from the river on the LNWR's Coalport branch opened in 1861 to link into the company's Wellington-Stafford line at Hadley Junction. The Wellington-Stafford line had been built, of course, by the Shropshire Union Railway. The LNWR also supplied the Coalport chinaworks factory with coal and china clay, as well as carrying away its

Above:
The official notice announcing the withdrawal of passenger trains north of Bewdley on display at Bridgnorth station in 1963.
Mrs M. Rutter

Right:
The remains of Ironbridge & Broseley station in 1966.
Selwyn Pearce Higgins (1966/45), National Railway Museum

Above:
The remains of Hampton Loade signalbox on 24 June 1967. Fortunately the preservation society prevented complete demolition. *Andrew Muckley*

nationally renowned products, all of which might have been channelled onto the Severn Valley Railway's proposed Coalport branch.

The 17 years between promotion and opening ensured that the Severn Valley Railway failed to capture any significant traffic from the River Severn. Between 1845 and 1862, river traffic was in rapid decline, and what trade the railway did win from the bargees and trow owners in the 1860s was but a fraction of what it might have secured 17 years earlier. All the railway really achieved ultimately was the commercial destruction of the last remains of a once nationally important trade artery.

The first few decades were lean years for the Severn Valley line, launched into a stagnant national economy in the 1860s followed by an agricultural depression in the 1870s. Almost no improvements were attempted on the branch until the 1880s. Only then and up to the first decade of the 20th century were any significant changes apparent. By then, every railway throughout the country was doing well, having become an accepted and essential part of the nation's economy by holding an almost complete monopoly of inland transport. Traders, manufacturers and the travelling public all complained about this monopoly, but branch lines such as the Severn Valley seemed finally to be secure and prosperous. It was during this period that money was available to update most of the signalling on the branch and to extend many of the station buildings (for example Arley in 1892 and again in 1901, and Highley in 1901 and 1904).

But the halcyon days, as they have often been called, were short-lived. There was

Above:
On the same day, Bridgnorth station shows signs of new life. *Andrew Muckley*

virtually no further investment in infrastructure, which remained unchanged until the line closed. Although railway photographs between the 1890s and World War 1 show beautifully manicured stations, proud uniformed staff, and immaculately turned out locomotives, revenue was being threatened by road competition. Stourport felt the effects first when the Kidderminster & Stourport Electric Tramway started to operate a service to and from these towns on 23 May 1898. No railway company at the time could have guessed how destructive to their operation roads would ultimately become, but with what appeared uncanny foresight, the GWR did look at its traffic receipts and realise the tram service was a threat and in January 1905 a frequent steam railmotor shuttle service was introduced between Bewdley, Kidderminster and Stourport. Two single-platform 'halts' were also opened especially for this new service. Foley Park Halt was situated a mile from Kidderminster exactly where the Kidderminster & Stourport Electric Tramway lines crossed the railway on a bridge. Rifle Range Halt (opened in June 1905) was a mile from Bewdley, but was not so logically positioned, and unlike Foley Park that lasted until the line closed in 1970, it closed at the beginning of October 1920.

After the war, the GWR tried a number of positive initiatives to attract people to the Severn Valley line. In 1913 it had published an attractive little booklet entitled *The Severn Valley*, one of its 'Handy Aids' series and this was reprinted during the 1920s. The second edition appeared in 1923 as No 7 of a set of eight, including *The Cornish Riviera* (No 1), *Devon — The Lovely Land of the Mayflower* (No 2) and the ambiguously titled *Cornwall and its Wild Life* (No 8). The GWR also produced posters encouraging people to travel to many of the beauty spots it served, including Shropshire and the Severn Valley. Special excursions and fishermen's trains were run, but passenger traffic continued to dwindle. In the 1930s the company was still prepared to innovate and it opened a number of new single-platform halts along the line, served by single-carriage auto-trains. But even this initiative could not stem the decline in passenger numbers.

The loss of ticket revenue was particularly marked at Bridgnorth and Berrington. At the former the number of tickets issued annually in the 15 years between 1923 and 1938 dropped by 66% from 40,127 to just 13,500. At Berrington during the same period the figures declined from 9,014 to 3,348. The cause of this dramatic fall was without a doubt direct competition from bus services, most of them operated by the Birmingham & Midland Motor Omnibus Co Ltd, better known as Midland Red. This firm's buses connected Bridgnorth with Ironbridge, Buildwas, Much Wenlock, and even Kidderminster (service No 297/8), a journey to the latter in 1939 advertised to take just an hour, a similar train journey taking no more than 45min. In the 1930s six GWR trains in each direction called at Berrington station every day except Sundays when there was just one up and one down train. Between the railway station and the county town the journey took 10-13min. By 1930 Midland Red ran 11 return journeys every Saturday between Shrewsbury and the village of Cross Houses and the hospital there, both within 2min walking distance of the railway station which was half a mile from the village of Berrington itself. Every day apart from Sundays and Mondays there were three return buses all taking approximately 23min to complete a single journey. Just before the outbreak of World War 2 this journey time had been reduced to 18min, by which time there were 17 return services on Saturdays, nine on Sundays, six on Wednesdays, four on Thursdays and Fridays and three on Tuesdays. With the bus service so superior to that offered by the railway, especially at weekends, there can be no doubt why ticket sales at Berrington station fell so dramatically in this period.

The Midland Red bus company also competed with the GWR for passengers at the southern end of the Severn Valley line but there the railway offered stiffer resistance. The first motorbus services to affect the railway in this area had been inaugurated between Kidderminster and Bewdley and Kidderminster and Stourport in November 1913, both routes operated by the Allen Motor Omnibus Co Ltd. The latter route competed directly with tram services operated by the Kidderminster & Stourport Electric Tramway Co, and so that company had also started to run its own motorbus service. In 1914 the rival undertakings were brought together as part of the Worcestershire Electric Traction Co Ltd.

The tramway between Kidderminster and Stourport was taken out of use on 30 November 1928. By then those early bus services had been taken over by Midland Red and new vehicles purchased to maintain them. In 1930 its No 291 service offered frequent journeys between Kidderminster and Bewdley, every half hour between 10.30am and 3.30pm, the trip lasting just under 20min. Between Kidderminster and Stourport there was a frequent 15min journey throughout the day, buses advertised to connect with various train services at Kidderminster railway station. By 1939 these journey times had not changed appreciably but between Kidderminster and Bewdley the timings had been cut to just 13min. However, if a passenger travelled by train between Kidderminster and Bewdley the journey could last as little as 10min, and as the trains were also frequent, the GWR managed to retain its share of customers between the two towns. In 1930 88,763 tickets were issued at Bewdley, and in 1938, 60,251, a decline of 33%. At Stourport the comparable figures for the same years were 18,510 and 16,269, a drop of only 12%.

Freight was traditionally more remunerative than passenger traffic, but even this was lost to road hauliers between the wars. It was during this period that access to stations and railway yards began to appear awkward when compared with 'door-to-door' lorry delivery and collection services. For example, in 1934 the Iron Bridge was closed to vehicular traffic, which meant any goods arriving at the station for the town only a stone's throw away had to be taken on a circular detour of a mile to make use of the nearest alternative river crossing.

By 1937 the Worcester Division of the GWR was trying unsuccessfully to win back traffic by reducing its rates. It was particularly concerned that it could not persuade the firms making clay roofing tiles at Jackfield to return to rail and throughout the summer of 1937 the Traffic Research Committee was reporting that clay extracted from the area was still being sent in bags by lorry to Tunstall despite initiatives to win it back to the railway.

After World War 2 traffic continued to ebb away. Between Ironbridge and Coalport, all clay and tile traffic was lost completely by the 1950s. Coalport Tileries stopped making roofing tiles in 1956, the decorative tile manufacturers, Craven Dunnill, had moved away from Jackfield to Bridgnorth immediately after the war and in April 1958 Jackfield sidings were officially taken out of use, followed at the end of 1959 by Maw & Co's sidings. An indication of just how much traffic had been lost to the railways in this area can be judged by the closure of Ironbridge & Broseley signalbox on 25 November 1956, one of only a few boxes to be taken out of use before the line closed as a through route. What had once been one of the busiest sections on the Severn Valley line had become the quietest.

During the same period passenger numbers continued to fall. Sunday passenger trains north of Bridgnorth were discontinued after the war. When photographing on the Severn Valley line during the 1950s, Michael Mensing noted on one print of a three-coach steam-hauled train: 'Not a single passenger on board!'. Inconvenience had become an issue. The majority of stations on the Severn Valley line were either on the wrong side of the river to the populations they were intended to serve (for example Ironbridge, Arley and Bewdley) or had inconvenient road access (for example Buildwas and Bridgnorth). The ferry connecting the village of Arley with the railway station operated until 1972 when a pedestrian bridge was opened across the river. In the 1860s access was a minor problem to a population used to a slower pace of life and the necessity of walking long distances to work. The railway then really was the fastest mode of transport once you were on the train. But to a post-World War 2 generation beginning to look for convenience in everything from washing machines to public transport, how easy a station was to reach regardless of how fast the train service was, was increasingly important. In the end, the railway was just not as attractive as a bus service which went through the middle of your town or village even if the journey might be longer than by train. And better still, of course, was the convenience of your own car parked outside your own front door ready to take you anywhere you wanted at a moment's notice.

The following are the weekday through services extracted from the timetables of October 1935, October 1945, August 1955 and September 1962:

October 1935

Worcester	7.05am	9.42	12.50	3.26pm	
Kidderminster (d)					5.46
Bewdley (d)	7.52	10.55	2.03	4.54	6.00
Bridgnorth (d)	8.25	11.28	2.43	5.32	6.42
Shrewsbury	9.21	12.15	3.35	6.28	7.37

Shrewsbury	8.15	11.25	1.50	5.30	7.50
Bridgnorth (d)	9.19	12.25	2.48	6.34	8.48
Bewdley (d)		1.00	3.20	7.10	9.39*
Kidderminster	9.56				
Worcester		1.50	4.17SO+	8.22	10.04

*9.55 SO +SX terminated at Hartlebury 3.34
An extra SO service left Shrewsbury at 10.30pm to arrive Kidderminster at 12pm
Sunday service: Kidderminster (d) 8.30am — Shrewsbury (a) 10.30; Shrewsbury (d) 4.50pm — Kidderminster (a) 6.43

October 1945

Worcester	7.00	12.53	5.20
Bewdley (d)	7.53	2.06	6.43
Bridgnorth (d)	8.28	2.42	7.21
Shrewsbury (a)	9.21	3.42	8.18

Shrewsbury (d)	8.15	11.05	5.30	8.45
Bridgnorth (d)	9.34	12.14	6.32	10.01
Bewdley (a)	10.05	12.52	7.05	10.32
Worcester (a)	-	1.55	-	11.10

August 1955

Worcester	6.55	12.45SX/1.15SO	5.30
Bewdley (d)	7.53	2.24	6.45
Bridgnorth (d)	8.30	2.59	7.20
Shrewsbury (a)	9.21	3.58	8.17
Shrewsbury	8.15	11.25	3.50
Bridgnorth (d)	9.34	12.13	4.49
Bewdley (d)	10.06	12.55	5.22
Worcester	-	1.46	(5.41)

September 1962

Hartlebury	7.00am		2.4*	4.10*	6.22
Kidderminster (d)		10.45*	2.05+	4.23+	
Bewdley (d)	7.16	10.55*	2.21	4.35	6.39
Bridgnorth (d)	7.55	11.35*	2.55	5.25	7.27
Shrewsbury	8.52	12.36*	3.54	6.37	8.26
Shrewsbury	1.45pm	4.20			
Bridgnorth (d)	3.04	5.20			
Bewdley (d)	3.43	5.57			
Kidderminster	3.52+				
Hartlebury	3.56*	6.11			

*SO, +SX

The Severn Valley line was simply not justifying its continued existence, and in June 1962 the Western Region of British Railways announced that passenger trains between Shrewsbury and Bewdley would be withdrawn, and the service south of Bewdley to Hartlebury and Kidderminster would be reduced. This announcement came at a time when every branch line throughout the country was under the closest scrutiny in the run-up to the publication of the British Transport Commission's report The Reshaping of British Railways. For the sake of historical accuracy it must be remembered that this publication, which will be forever remembered as 'The Beeching Report', appeared on 27 March 1963, nine months after the announcement to withdraw passenger services north of Bewdley. Bridgnorth Town Council objected to these proposals and stated that it believed the line could be promoted as a 'holiday attraction'. On 8 November 1962 the Transport Users Consultative Committee (TUCC) organised a public meeting at Bridgnorth to test local opinion and after that meeting it wrote to the British Transport Commission (BTC) objecting that closure would mean:

a) hardship to rail users in Bridgnorth and Highley

b) definite hardship to people of Apley Forge and to old-age pensioners in rural communities

c) hardship to anglers and weekend visitors to the Severn Valley.

With the best will in the world, these arguments against closure were far from convincing. It was sad that Mr Philip Shaw of Morville Heath feared he would go out of business if he could no longer send his day-old chicks from Bridgnorth station (between July 1960 and June 1961 he had dispatched 537 boxes), but it was not the sort of appeal likely to change the heart of the Minister of Transport. Another objector was a Mr W. H. Garbett of Coalbrookdale who travelled regularly by train from Ironbridge & Broseley station to Shrewsbury. His objection to closure was also an ineffectual lone voice, but he is mentioned here because during the 1960s he lived in the house next door to where the present author is writing this book!

These objections obviously carried little weight and the statistics gathered by the officials working on the Beeching Report in September 1962 only strengthened the arguments for closure. During that month, only 70 singles and 194 special cheap day returns were issued at Ironbridge for Shrewsbury. Thirteen Ironbridge and Coalbrookdale residents were regular passengers on the 8.17am train arriving in the county town at 8.52am but it was said that the daily 8.05am Midland Red bus service between Ironbridge and Shrewsbury (arriving at 8.45 and taking only 5min more than the train journey to the county town) was better patronised. Between Bridgnorth and Shrewsbury 11 school-children travelled regularly during the week on the 7.57am train and 10 female office workers travelled regularly from Highley on the 8.16am train to Kidderminster.

The BTC was obviously unmoved and in August 1963 the official notice of withdrawal of passenger services north of Bewdley was announced to come into effect on 9 September 1963. Freight and parcels traffic continued until the end of the year, after which time only coal traffic to and from Alveley Colliery was dealt with. Bridgnorth Borough and District Councils were apparently taken by surprise at the withdrawal of freight services and were moved to write directly to Dr Beeching and the then Leader of the Opposition, Harold Wilson MP, soon to be the new Prime Minister.

Left:
As preservation took hold between Bridgnorth and Eardington in the late 1960s, at the south end of the Severn Valley line British Rail maintained its passenger service to Bewdley and Stourport. In this photograph, the 16.42 Hartlebury-Bewdley train stops briefly at Stourport in driving snow on 7 February 1969. *J. G. Glover*

Above:
Bewdley station in January 1970 in the final days of British Rail ownership. *Andrew Muckley*

Amazingly, Wilson actually replied to the Town Clerk at Bridgnorth on 27 November 1963, the letter (a polite but bland reply) still preserved in the Shropshire Records & Research Centre, Shrewsbury. From 2 December 1963 all Severn Valley line stations except Bewdley and Stourport closed completely. Officially, that is, because parts of the Severn Valley clung to life just long enough to allow the preservationists to establish a foothold.

Track was quickly taken up between Buildwas and Bridgnorth but Mr Elias Thorpe still kept his licensed refreshment room open within the station buildings there despite the lack of trains. Fortunately the track southwards from Bridgnorth to Alveley Colliery remained intact long enough for negotiations between British Railways and the Severn Valley Railway Society to successfully culminate in the purchase by the latter of this stretch of line on 1 January 1967. The line north of Buildwas was abandoned between 1965 and 1968, with only a short section retained south of Sutton Bridge Junction, Shrewsbury, to provide a connection to an oil depot on the site of the former Potteries railway station opposite Shrewsbury Abbey. The section between Alveley and Bewdley was officially closed by British Railways on 3 February 1969, followed on 5 January 1970 by the withdrawal of the passenger service between Bewdley, Kidderminster and Hartlebury. The remains of the branch struggled on for another decade and then on 12 January 1981 the line between

Hartlebury Junction and Stourport power station was taken out of use, followed in February 1984 by closure of the section between Kidderminster Junction and British Sugar's Kidderminster factory.

By then the Severn Valley Railway Society was firmly established as a professional and highly respected railway operator, and it came as no surprise that at the very end of July 1984, steam-hauled passenger trains were once again running from Bridgnorth via Bewdley into Kidderminster, albeit to a new terminal station. Due to the efforts of those dedicated Severn Valley Railway volunteers, almost half the length of the original Severn Valley line is still in use, the trains carrying considerably more passengers than at any time in the branch line's history. They may be tourists and only travelling for enjoyment, but at least part of the Severn Valley line still has a future.

WEST MIDLAND—SEVERN VALLEY.

DOWN TRAINS		1 2	1 2 8	1 2	1 2 3	Sun
Hartlebury. *Dep*	..	8 18	9 35	2 35	6 55	9 40
Stourport	..	8 26	9 48	2 44	7 3	9 48
Bewdley	..	8 34	9 58	2 55	7 15	9 56
Bridgnorth	..	9 4	1050	8 32	7 55	1034
Linley	..	9 18	11 6	A	A	1046
Coalport	—	9 20	1116	3 47	8 10	1053
Ironbridge	..	9 25	1122	3 53	8 15	1059
Buildwas.	...	9 30	1140	4 0	8 20	11 4
Wenlock *dep*	..	8 15	10 3	3 40	7 10	7 30
arr.	..	1025	1152	5 12	9 29	..
Cressage	...	9 39	1149	4 10	8 29	1114
Berrington	.	9 47	1158	A	8 33	1124
Shrewsbury *Arr*	...	9 57	12 8	4 30	8 48	1135

A—Stops when required.

UP TRAINS.	1 2 3	1 2	1 2	1 2 3	Sun
Shrewsbury *Dep*	6 55	11 5	3 30	6 55	5 5
Berrington	7 5	1115	3 40	7	5 15
Cressage	7 15	1125	3 50	7 1	5 25
Wenlock *dep.*	..	10 3	3 40	7 10	..
arr.	1025	1152	5 12	7 50	8 40
Buildwas	7 26	1140	4 2	7 29	5 35
Ironbridge	7 35	1145	4 8	7 33	5 40
Coalport	7 40	1150	4 14	7 38	5 45
Linley	7 47	1158	4 22	A	5 52
Bridgnorth	7 59	1210	4 36	7 54	6 4
Bewdley	8 45	1254	5 17	8 29	6 40
Stourport	8 55	1 8	5 28	8 38	6 50
Hartlebury *Arr.*	9 5	1 18	5 34	8 48	7 0

SEVERN VALLEY.

	am	am	am	pm	pm	pm	pm	pm (Sun.)	pm (Sun.)
Shrewsbury	..	8 30	1125	..	3 45	5 30	7 12	..	..
Berrington.	..	8 41	1135	..	3 57	5 40	7 25	..	..
Cressage ..	..	8 50	1145	..	4 5	5 47	7 34	..	..
Buildwas ..	..	9 6	12 2	..	4 22	5 55	7 41	..	..
Iron-Bridge	..	9 11	12 7	..	4 28	6 2	7 57	..	..
Coalport ..	..	9 16	1212	..	4 33	6 8	8 2	..	..
Linley	..	9 22	1218	..	4 39	6 15	8 8	..	..
Bridgnorth.	7 10	9 29	1225	1 25	4 47	6 23	8 15	6 5	..
Eardington	7 16	9 38	1234	1 33	4 58	6 36	..	..	..
Hampton L	7 21	9 43	1239	1 39	5 4	6 41	9 36	6 16	..
Highley ..	7 27	9 49	1245	1 45	5 10	6 47	9 43	6 23	..
Arley	7 33	9 55	1251	1 52	5 16	6 53	9 50	6 30	..
Bewdley ..	7 40	10 2	1258	2 1	5 23	7 0	9 59	6 38	..
Worcester	8 52	1052	1 50	3 22	6 23	8 8	1117	7 30	..
	am	**am**	**am**	**pm**	**pm**	**pm**	**pm**	**am**	**am**
Worcester	7 20	9 47	1040	1254	2 28	4 5	6 59	..	9 20
Bewdley ..	8 5	1034	1130	2 6	3 25	5 4	7 40	..	10 9
Arley	8 12	1043	1138	2 14	3 33	5 17	7 49	..	1018
Highley ...	8 20	1050	1144	2 21	3 40	5 23	7 55	..	1024
Hampton L	8 25	1056	1150	2 27	3 46	5 28	8 0	..	1029
Eardington.	8 30	11 1	1156	2 32	3 52	5 33	8 5	..	..
Bridgnorth.	8 39	1112	12 2	2 41	4 1	5 42	8 30	..	1033
Linley	8 47	1121	..	2 49	4 10	5 50	8 38	..	..
Coalport ..	8 53	1128	..	2 55	4 17	5 56	8 44	..	..
Iron-Bridge	8 59	1135	..	3 1	4 26	6 5	8 50	..	..
Buildwas ..	9 8	1138	..	3 8	4 32	6 16	8 54	..	..
Cressage ...	9 17	1153	..	3 14	4 40	6 25	9 2	..	..
Berrington	9 26	12 1	..	3 22	4 50	6 35	9 8	..	..
Shrewsbury	9 40	1215	..	3 33	5 1	6 45	9 21	..	..

Above:
Timetable for West Midland -Severn Valley from 3 February 1872

Left:
Severn Valley timetable dated 27 January 1912.

Acknowledgements and Bibliography

As the title of this book suggests, the emphas is pictorial — a view from the past. The author has tried hard to select from the very limited number of photographs available, images that reflect all aspects of that past — the people, trains, and locations. In helping to achieve this balance, special thanks go to David Postle, curator of the Kidderminster Railway Museum and long-serving stationmaster at the preserved Severn Valley Railway station at Highley. He gave the author invaluable and unselfish help in the quest for images. Thanks also go to Mrs Viggars and her son-in-law Mr Pearson for allowing the author to borrow and copy original photographs; Michael Mensing for responding so promptly to requests for photographs; Russell Mulford, Shrewsbury; Neil Clarke, Little Wenlock; Ron Miles, Jackfield; Rex Key, Broseley; Ed Bartholomew, National Railway Museum; Brian Moone, Kidderminster; Lens of Sutton; F. W. Shuttleworth, Ludlow; Ken Jones, Little Wenlock; John Powell, Ironbridge Gorge Museum; David Houlston, Wellington; Mrs Rutter, Bridgnorth. The author also wishes to thank staff at the following institutions — Shropshire Records & Research, Stourport Library, Worcestershire Record Office, and Kidderminster Library.

As well as contemporary sources, the following have been used in the preparation of this book.

Tony Barfield, 'Great Western Locomotives on the Severn Valley', *Severn Valley Railway News*, No 25, autumn 1972, pp12-15
K. M. Beck, *The West Midlands Lines of the Great Western Railway*, Ian Allan, 1983
Keith Beddoes & William H. Smith, *The Tenbury & Bewdley Railway*, Wild Swan, 1995
Paul Collins, *Rail Centres: Wolverhampton*, Ian Allan, 1990
R. A. Cooke, *Track Layout Diagrams of the Great Western Railway*, Section 32, East Shropshire, 2nd edition, 1994
Barrie Geens, *The Severn Valley Railway at Arley*, Wild Swan, revised edition, 1995
Great Western Railway, *The Severn Valley*, Handy Aids No 7, 1st edition 1913, (2nd edition 1923)
G. Hurst, *Register of Closed Railways 1948-91*, Milepost, 1992
John Marshall, *The Severn Valley Railway*, David St John Thomas, 1989
Richard K. Morriss, *Rail Centres: Shrewsbury*, Ian Allan, 1986
A. J. Mugridge, *A Short History of William Exley & Sons*, published by the author, 1997
Sir Gerald Nabarro, MP, *Severn Valley Steam*, Routledge & Kegan Paul, 1971
Nikolaus Pevsner, *The Buildings of England: Shropshire* 1974, & *Worcestershire*, Penguin, 1968
D. J. Smith, *The Severn Valley Railway*, Town & Country Press, 1968
Michael Stratton, *Ironbridge and The Electric Revolution*, John Murray in association with National Power, 1994
John Tennant, 'The Billingsley and Kinlet Railways', *Severn Valley Railway News*, No 24, summer 1972, pp23-27
Barrie Trinder, *The Industrial Revolution in Shropshire*, Phillimore, 1973